# The New Jerusalem    Planning and Politics

View from the Mount of Olives across the Old City to the west Jerusalem skyline.

Arthur Kutcher

# The New Jerusalem

Planning and Politics

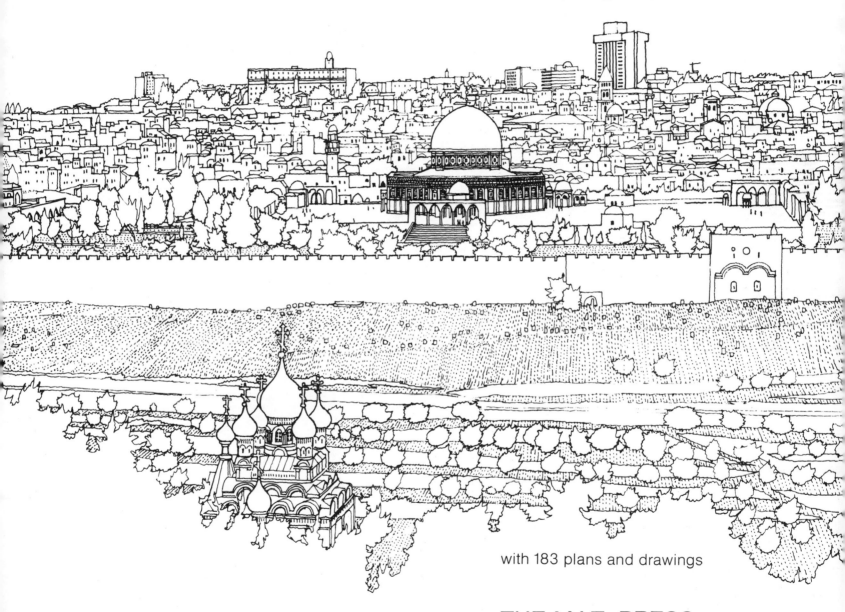

with 183 plans and drawings

THE M.I.T. PRESS

Cambridge, Massachusetts

Foreword by Vincent Scully

First American Edition, 1975,
published by The MIT Press

Printed and Bound in the United States of America

Library of Congress Catalog Card Number 74-10483
ISBN No. 0-262-11058-X (hardcover)
ISBN No. 0-262-61020-5 (paperback)

# Contents

# Foreword

In this pure and beautiful book Arthur Kutcher, who has already become a symbol of civic responsibility in Jerusalem, puts his intense professional competence to the service of human reverence and love. This is the way experts and humanists should but rarely do function in the modern world. Kutcher's competence is that of a trained architect who has taught himself how to see, how to perceive the relationships between things, and finally how to draw them so that other people can see them and perceive their meaning too. Kutcher's love is for the city of Jerusalem in its sacred landscape – now, so he claims, being disastrously built up and destroyed. Despite his subtitle, Kutcher's approach is not fundamentally political. There should be no comfort in his book for the enemies of Israel. The mistakes it describes are being made all over the world today, as modern mass humanity moves – inexorably so far – toward the destruction of its earth, of its balanced environment, and of its sacred places everywhere. Kutcher points out, for example, that some of the most mindlessly obtrusive luxury hotels in Jerusalem were built under Jordanian rule.

The main divisions of his argument are especially sympathetic and convincing to me for a number of reasons. The first two chapters analyze the forms of the city in relation to those of its landscape and describe its special character as a sacred place in those terms. My own work on Greek temples in landscape leads me to believe that this method is the right one, and that the various scholarly groups which should have perceived and understood the importance of those relationships, and which should have defended them against expedient decisions, failed Jerusalem exactly as their counterparts in Greece failed Athens in a visual and, eventually, a political way. 'Mole-like the devout scour the site for sacred relics, never sensing Jerusalem's natural grandeur', Kutcher writes. It sounds like a typical archaeological sherding expedition in Attica, or perhaps anywhere, while the commercial developers lurk in the wings, 'hand on the bulldozer's throttle . . . waiting their chance.' So the Hilton Hotels in Athens and Jerusalem alike came into being, and any number of other grossly conceived high-rises to exploit the site, destroy its man-nature relationships, and smash its scale. But much more happened, and Kutcher describes how the long series of twentieth-century planning schemes for Jerusalem culminated in the Master Plan of 1968 which, though containing some humane features, was based in large part upon the cataclysmic principles of Ville Radieuse unitary formalism, with enormous superhighways, interchanges, and connectors, intended to take over the landscape and to smash their way through the city in order to serve a new and dense commercial core. Now it all begins to sound to me like Urban Redevelopment in the United States during the 1950s and '60s as I wrote about it during the latter decade.

At this point Kutcher becomes perhaps obsessively professional, and his Chapter III deals at some length with how the architects and planners of what he correctly calls the 'know-nothing' generation, arrogant and insensitive, got to be the awful way they are. His attack upon their doctrinaire model for action, which is in fact a kind of deterministic 'modern' historicism, echoes similar views expressed in the 1960s by people as otherwise divergent as Robert Venturi, Colin Rowe, and myself. So I cannot help but be interested in this more general and theoretical part of the book, and I respect Kutcher's determination to develop its theme. It finally gets back to Jerusalem in exactly the right way, by trying to show us how we can break through these worn-out abstract preconceptions in order to see the city in its landscape as it really is and might properly and integrally be.

Kutcher's last chapter reads exactly like what happened in New Haven, Conn., USA, in the 1960s. It is true that the Master Plan was rejected in Jerusalem, as it was not in New Haven, but the major principle in both cities came to be the typical Urban Redevelopment one of the attraction of money to the place: hence luxury flats and hotels, very little low-income housing, massive concessions to developers, and (apparently much more in Jerusalem than in New Haven, though not than in Athens, it must be said) the waiving of zoning restrictions, if any, in the speculators' favour. A veteran of the old skirmishes of the 1960s cannot read about this new engagement of the 1970s without considerable emotion, even some awe. In a sense, it is all *déjà vu*, old stuff; hard to believe that it is still going on. But it is indeed going on. And now the struggle has come to the very heart of the matter: to the ultimate Holy City itself, not only the living capital of a nation sorely beset but the symbolic home of a great portion of mankind. And right here, as we learned in those old wars, is where the politics must come in, and where the practising architects (or most of them, there are always courageous exceptions) normally fail most dismally, and where it is finally public pressure democratically applied – as it most emphatically still can be in New Haven and Jerusalem alike, and perhaps now even in Athens – which begins to save the city and to form principles for new buildings as they ought to take shape in the specific place. Here in this last act we cannot help but be aware again of what a good man Kutcher is. He is sometimes angry but never rabid. He has his share of irony, and he recognizes the humanity in politicians, too, and likes them pretty well, especially the Mayor of Jerusalem, it seems. He fights straight and rough with them all, win a few lose a few, not like the self-righteous fanatic that the expert sometimes turns out to be in these cases, but like a civilized, resourceful man. I am enormously moved that Kutcher was a student of mine for a while some years ago. I am proud of him, and I admire this book.

VINCENT SCULLY

Yale University.

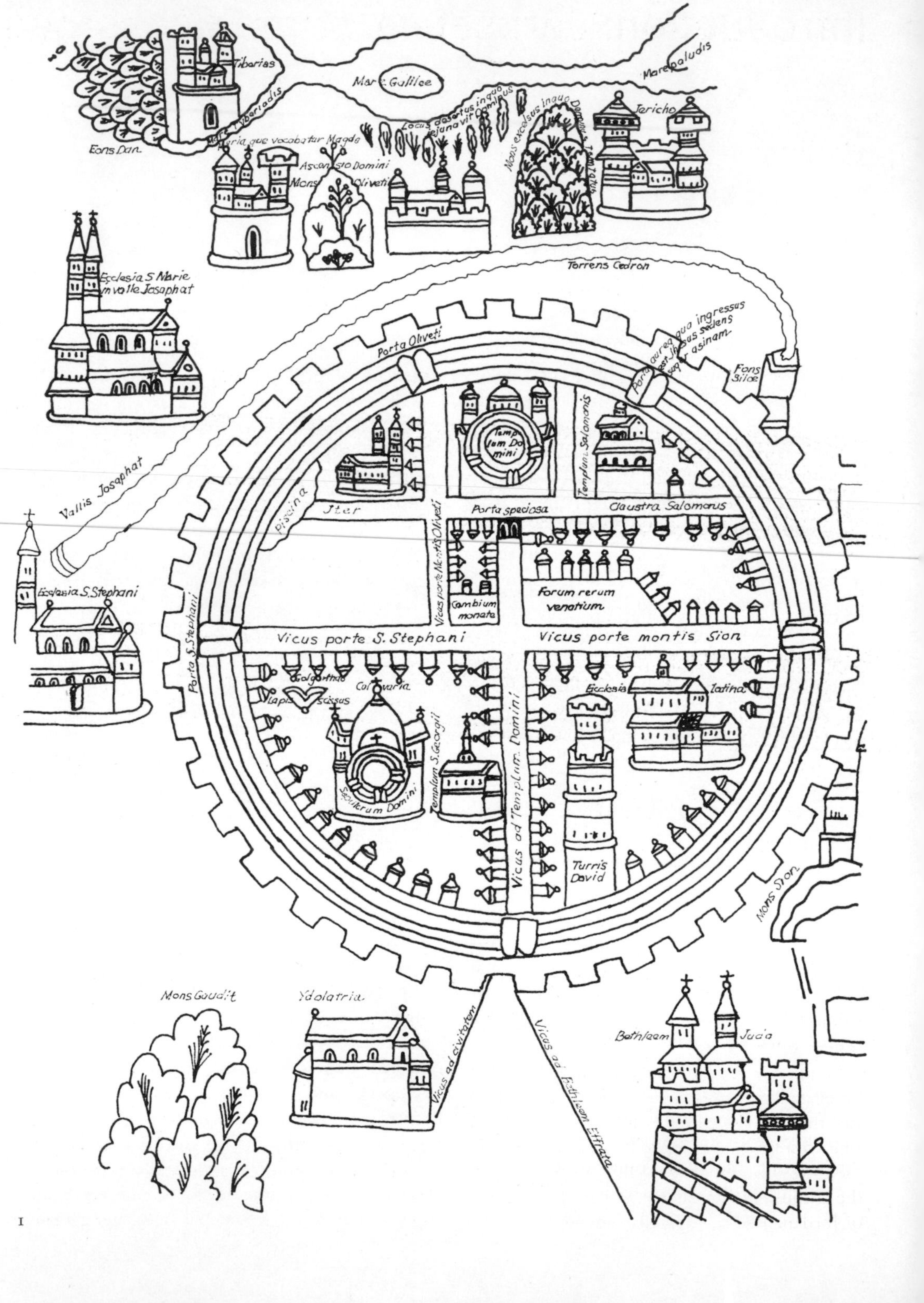
Tibarias
Mare Galilee
Mare paludis
Jericho
Fons Dan
Ascensio Domini
Mons Oliveti
Ecclesia S Marie
in valle Josaphat
Torrens Cedron
Porta Oliveti
Porta aurea qua ingressus est Jhesus sedens super asinam
Fons Siloe
Templum Domini
Templum Salomonis
Vallis Josaphat
piscina
Iter
Porta speciosa
Claustra Salomonis
Vicus porte Montis Oliveti
Ecclesia S. Stephani
Forum rerum venatium
Cambium monete
Vicus porte S. Stephani
Vicus porte montis Sion
Porta S. Stephani
Golgotha
Calvaria
Lapis scissus
Ecclesia
Latina
Templum S. Georgii
Sepulcrum Domini
Vicus ad Templum Domini
Turris David
Mons Sion
Mons Gaudii
Ydolatria
Vicus ad civitatem
Vicus ad Bethleem Effrata
Bethleem
Juda

1 Crusader Jerusalem and its environs, after a twelfth century map.

# Introduction: Jerusalem at the Crossroads

TRADITIONALLY CONSIDERED the centre of the earth, Jerusalem does indeed lie geographically and culturally on a line dividing East and West. In the course of her four-thousand-year history, the city has passed from the domain of the Eastern world to that of the West, and back again. In our own lifetime, Jerusalem is undergoing the most recent, and perhaps most fateful, of those great, often cataclysmic shifts of orientation which have stamped her history.

From its beginning in the Bronze Age until the third century BC, the city lay within the cultural sphere of the Semitic peoples, spiritually and politically a part of Asia. The first great change in her orientation occurred at the time of the conquests of Alexander the Great; for the next thousand years, Jerusalem would belong to the West, to the Hellenistic, Roman, and Byzantine worlds. The rule of the West was ended by the Islamic conquest in the year 638. Except for the brief interlude of the Crusades in the twelfth century, Jerusalem remained in the sphere of the Orient for nearly thirteen hundred years. In 1917 the British, under General Allenby, took the city from the Turks. But although the British Mandatory Government nominally brought Jerusalem under Western influence, she remained in her cultural and economic life a provincial Middle-eastern town.

In 1948, with the founding of the State of Israel and the subsequent war between Israel and the Arab States, the city was cut in half. The western part became the capital of Israel; the eastern part with the Old City came under the administration of the Hashemite Kingdom of Jordan. The divided city languished.'

The Israeli victory in June 1967 reunified Jerusalem. It also brought contemporary Western culture in a massive dose. The speed and magnitude of the cultural and technological changes which are now occurring are far greater than any in Jerusalem's past. There can be no doubt that the next few years will stamp the city's character for decades, perhaps for centuries to come.

The question is of course what sort of values and ideals is Western civilization bringing to the Holy City? As a specific instance of a general case, Jerusalem presents one of the most extreme and hurtful examples of contemporary Western technology and Western values invading and clashing with a city whose form and setting are essentially pre-technological, a city relatively uncorrupted by contemporary urban ills, built according to principles and priorities totally at variance with those of our contemporary Western civilization. In the light of this fierce conflict, like the blazing and merciless light of the Jerusalem sun, one sees with stabbing clarity what in other places is still blurred: the moral and stylistic bankruptcy of modern architecture, and the suicidal impulses of contemporary town planning, 'trend planning', 'accommodating pressures', like a physician accommodating disease.

An old Zionist dictum says: 'If you will it, it is so'. There is a choice. It lies between building the New Jerusalem according to the principles of Baron Haussmann, or according to the principles of the prophet Isaiah. The one is a city manipulated to achieve certain political and economic ends, the other is the city as an affirmation of human values, and the promise of a spiritual reality. Lewis Mumford in his letter to the Jerusalem Committee explains the vision, the possibility, and the obligation: 'Jerusalem holds a special place as a holy city, not only because of its age, but because in time it became the active spiritual centre of three world religions. Thus it stands for certain cosmic insights and human values that have spread throughout the planet, and that now embrace, in some degree, all who consciously participate in the human adventure. This precious gift of history gives Jerusalem a status that no other sacred city, not even Mecca, Rome, Benares, or Constantinople can claim. Despite all present divisions and antagonisms, some now more fiercely visible than ever, the structure of the city, its topography, its soil, its ancient walls, its historic sites, make Jerusalem in its presence and person, a potential source of unity. . . . I feel that in Jerusalem not merely the fate of Israel, but the destiny of the world in the centuries to come may actually be at stake. Yet this, I take it, may be one of those singular moments of which the great physicist Clark Maxwell once wrote: "when an insignificant force, exerted at a propitious moment, may effect an enormous change which would otherwise be beyond human possibility."

Those moments do not occur often; and they are seldom perceived in time, and still more seldom acted upon. But to close one's eyes to this strategic moment for fear of giving offence to this or that group, whether weak or powerful, would do no service to Israel: in fact it would be a betrayal of the deepest aspirations of Judaism, long ago expressed by Isaiah.'

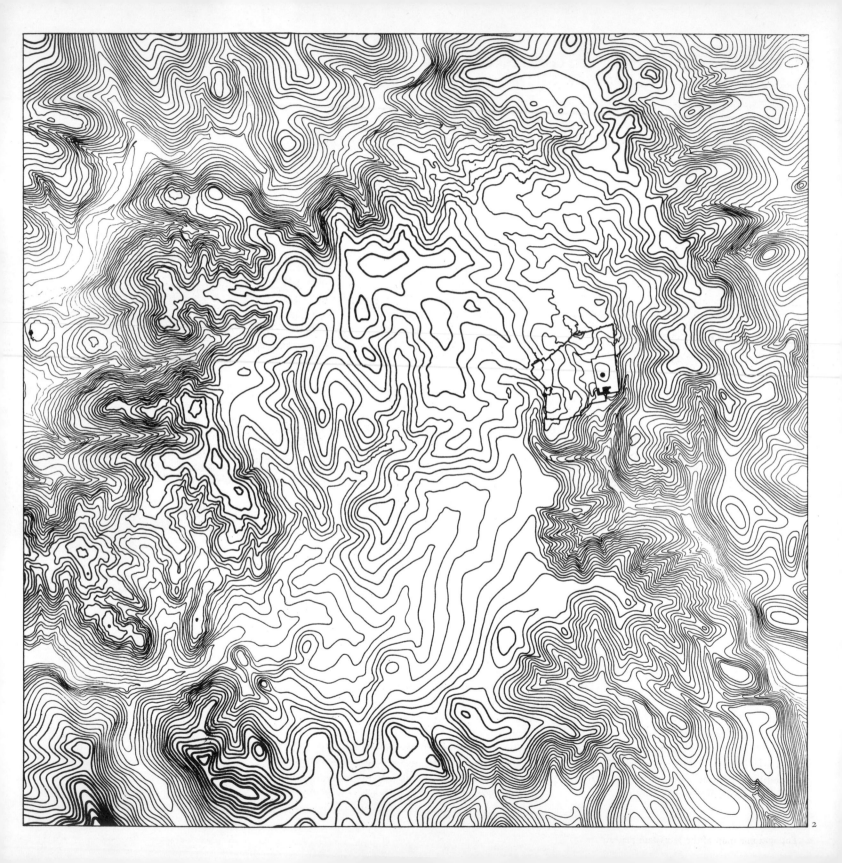

2

# I   The realities of the site

*'The hills stand about Jerusalem'*

FROM BEITIN in the north to the Valley of Beersheba in the south, the Judean Mountains form the backbone of the Holy Land. Mid-way along these mountains lie the Jerusalem Hills, a saddle between the Beit El Mountains and the Hebron Hills. The 'city space' of Jerusalem is a plateau on the main watershed of the Jerusalem Hills. The plateau is sharply defined by steep edges; within it the topography is gentler, consisting of softly domed hills and shallow valleys whose governing lines are horizontal. At the eastern side of the plateau, the Valley of Kidron together with the tributaries which form it, the Valleys of Hinnom (Gehenna) and Jehosaphat, have carved out a great basin with steep slopes, ringed by hills on three sides, opening out to the Judean Desert, like a harbour opening to the sea. Jutting into this 'harbour' is an extension of the Jerusalem plateau, somewhat lower than the hills surrounding it – the promontory of the Old City. Just to the north and west is the line of the watershed; to the west, drainage is toward the Mediterranean Sea, to the east, toward the Jordan valley. The Valley of Kidron starts at Jerusalem's mountain plateau, 2500 feet above sea level, and flows to the lowest point on the earth's surface, the Dead Sea, fourteen miles away. Kidron has its western mirror image in Emek Refaim (the Valley of the Ghosts), beginning a few hundred metres outside the Old City and leading to the Mediterranean Sea. The Old City basin also finds its mirror image, in a gentler form, in the central basin of West Jerusalem, site of Israel's government centre and of the Hebrew University.

The site of the Old City is an ancient crossing of the north-south trade route along the crest of the Judean Mountains with the east-west route from the Jordan valley to the Mediterranean coastal plain. Surrounded by steep slopes on three sides, easily defensible, with one of the rare springs in this part of Judea nearby, the site has been inhabited for at least the last four thousand years.

The Old City lies on the knife edge between the Mediterranean region and the desert, and her climate, geology, soils, and vegetation reflect this fact. The eastern boundary of the Jerusalem area is both a topographical and a climatic border: here the great plunge towards the Judean desert and the 400 mm rainfall line coincide. Two miles to the east of the Old City the line of less than 400 mm yearly rainfall connects the villages of Chizmeh and Anatot in the north and El Eyzaria and Abu-Dis in the south, marking the beginning of the vast Central Asian deserts. The line is known locally as the 'starvation line'.

Jerusalem's climate combines the short, mild, rainy winter of the Mediterranean region with the blazing summer sun of the arid highlands. With an extraordinarily high percentage of cloudless days, Jerusalem is one of the sunniest places on earth. As any Jerusalem photographer will tell you, her sky is incredibly bright, and of an astonishing colour, a deep cobalt blue. The extreme clarity of her mountain air, and the brightness of her sky can make distances hard to judge: near and far often appear juxtaposed, seemingly on the same plane.

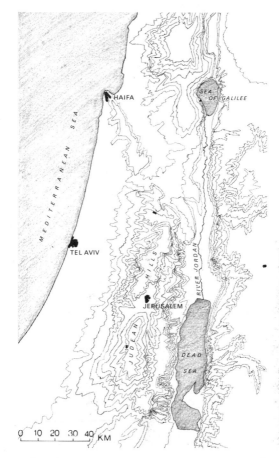

3  Location map.

4  The topographic structure of the Jerusalem plateau. A The Old City basin; B Line of the watershed; C Central basin of West Jerusalem.

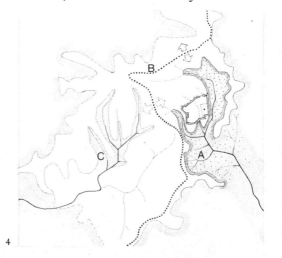

2  Topographic map of the Jerusalem plateau.

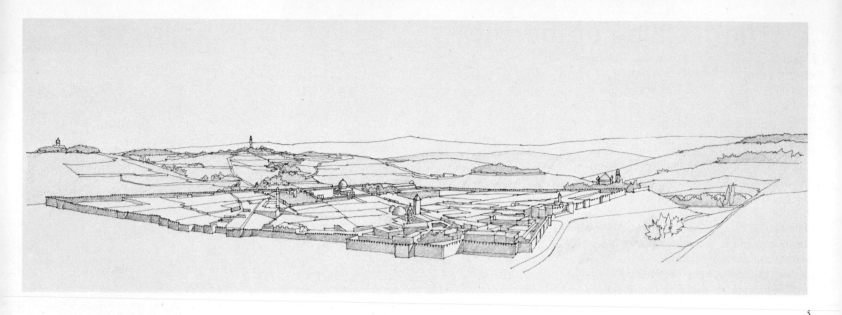

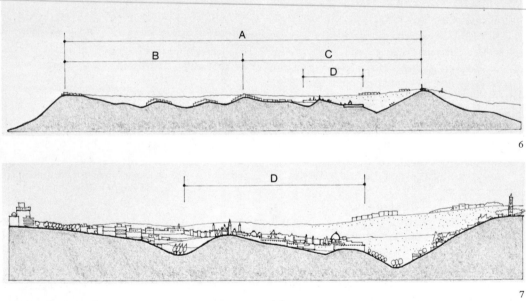

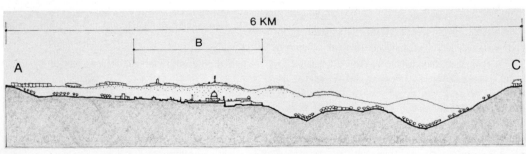

5  Aerial view from the north-east. The Old City sits in a bowl ringed by hills.

6  Section through the Jerusalem plateau looking north: A  The plateau; B  The Central basin; C  The Old City basin; D  The Old City.

7  Detail of 6 showing the Old City (D) and its surrounding hills.

8  Section looking east. A  French Hill; B  The Old City; C  The Mount of Evil Counsel.

The geologic structure of the area – a mixture of the terraced rhythms of the Mediterranean Region's Kenoman and Turonic limestones with the soft, chalky Senon strata of the desert – as well as the soils – the heavy brownish-red, fertile Terra Rosa of the west and the light, friable, greyish, barren Renzina of the desert – manifest the meeting of two great regions which characterize the city. In the basin of the Old City one sees them intermingling: opposite Mount Zion, in the 'Fields of Blood', the sheer, craggy faces of great stepped limestone slabs, once risen from the sea; on the hills of Abu-Dis, a few hundred metres away, the smooth, barren undulations of the Senon, the desert strata; on the Mount of Evil Counsel, in interwoven patches, the rich, heavy Terra Rosa with its carpet of delicate grasses, meeting the grey, chalky Renzina, hardly supporting life.

Jerusalem's vegetation reflects the fact that culturally the region is very old, having been inhabited for millennia. The natural vegetation of the western portion of the region, consisting of forests of live oak and deciduous pistachio, and of groves of Jerusalem pine, has been augmented by man with the planting of olive trees, cypresses, carobs, figs, pomegranates, almonds, and vineyards.

Until very recently, the man-made landscape in Jerusalem, particularly in the area of the Old City, followed a clear and impressive logic. Prominent hill tops, often the sites of monasteries or public institutions, were planted with dense groves of Jerusalem pine, giving shade and welcome shelter from the strong winds. When the soil and the presence of water permitted, olive trees were planted on the hillsides and in the shallower valleys. Those places in the valley bottoms where the run-off from winter rains could be easily collected became lush orchards and arbours. The rhythm of hill-tops emphasized by dark masses of pine, the red-earthed, terraced slopes, with their regular grid-pattern of olives, and the thick groves of fruit trees at key points in the valleys, all produced a simple, yet extremely powerful man-made counterpoint to the starkness and intricacy of the natural landscape, to the massive domes of its ancient hills, its faceted

slopes, and the delicate textures of its vegetation.

To the northern European and North American mind and eye, this is a profoundly alien landscape. Seeing it for the first time the Western foreigner often becomes uncomfortable, often wishes, understandably enough, that it be made a little less stark, a little less strange, a bit more congenial, and finally (and why not?), a lot more profitable. That is the way the world ends.

9 The Old City's visual space measures about 2 by 3 miles.

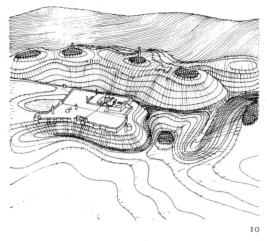

10

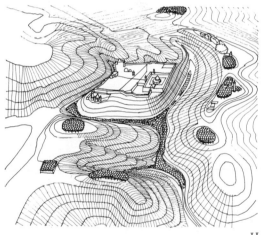

11

10 Diagrammatic view of the Old City's visual space from the west.

11 View from the south.

12 Geological section showing the relation of the rock strata to the topographical structure of the area.

12

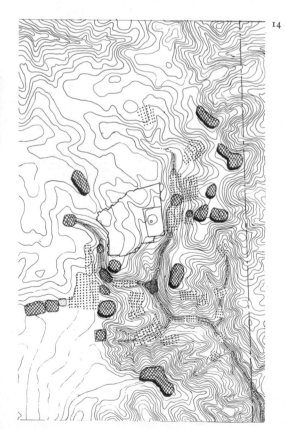

13  A view from Mount Zion towards the Judean Desert. Here the Mediterranean and desert landscapes intermingle.

14  The man-made landscape of the Old City area emphasizes hill tops and valley bottoms. The intermediate slopes are given a light carpet of olive trees.

15  The landscape of the Mediterranean region: a dense grove of Jerusalem pine in the Judean hills.

## The Old City and the Temple Mount

The physical character and strength of Jerusalem lie in her landscape – the light, the colours and textures, the rugged topography – and in the harmonious relation between the works of nature and man. Through the cumulative process of history, despite the numerous destructions, the built landscape of Jerusalem has harmonized with the natural fabric or has complemented the natural order with monuments respecting the scale and the essence of the place. Men from many cultures, Jews, Greeks, Romans, Arabs, Armenians, Frenchmen, Germans, Russians, Turks, Englishmen, have, until very recently, somehow known how and where to build, and equally important, how and where not to build.

The vernacular of building in Jerusalem is, or was until recently, an organic vernacular, which combined practicality in terms of climate, materials, and structure, with a strong feeling for the site. The elements of the vernacular are simple volumes and masses, plain wall surfaces with small openings, and subtle surface textures which break and soften the light. Architectural refinements are found in the treatment of window frames, shutter details, and the wrought-iron work of railings and grilles. The individual buildings might seem plain, even dowdy. But that hardly matters: it is not the individual building that counts here, but rather the ensemble, and the relation of the ensemble to the site. The uniform use of Jerusalem stone minimizes the distinction between individual buildings; the golden-red **Mizi Achmar** and cream-coloured Mizi Yahudi varieties of the Kenoman rock strata, and the Old City's Mizi Holi (Arabic for 'sweet stone' – because it is so easy to cut), are Jerusalem's building material; their colours blend softly with the tawny hills. Buildings and ensembles, composed of multiples of a four-metre cube, are ideally suited in scale and rhythm to follow the curves and slopes of Jerusalem's hills. Examples of ensembles are found throughout Jerusalem, in various nuclear groupings, reflecting the lives of the various cultures which inhabit them. The greatest and most compact collection of these ensembles is the Old City.

The present form of the Old City of Jerusalem derives the position of its walls and its basic division into quarters from the Roman legionary camp, Aelia Capitolina, built over the ruins of Jewish Jerusalem, destroyed by Titus in AD 70. The Old City's principal streets follow the alignment of the Roman cross-axes, the north-south *cardo*, and the east-west *decumanus*, found in all Roman military settlements. The dense fabric of buildings within the Old City, composed of introverted residential clusters roughly following a 70m × 70m grid, has its origins to a great extent in Crusader times with occasional traces of Byzantine and even Roman constructions still discernible.

16 A group of buildings inside the Jaffa Gate. Variations of the Jerusalem vernacular produce an architectural ensemble.

17 The Arab village of Silwan opposite the Old City on the east harmonizes with the landscape structure.

18 A view towards the Jewish settlement of Yemin Moshe outside the city walls on the west shows another kind of harmonious dialogue with the landscape.

16

17

18

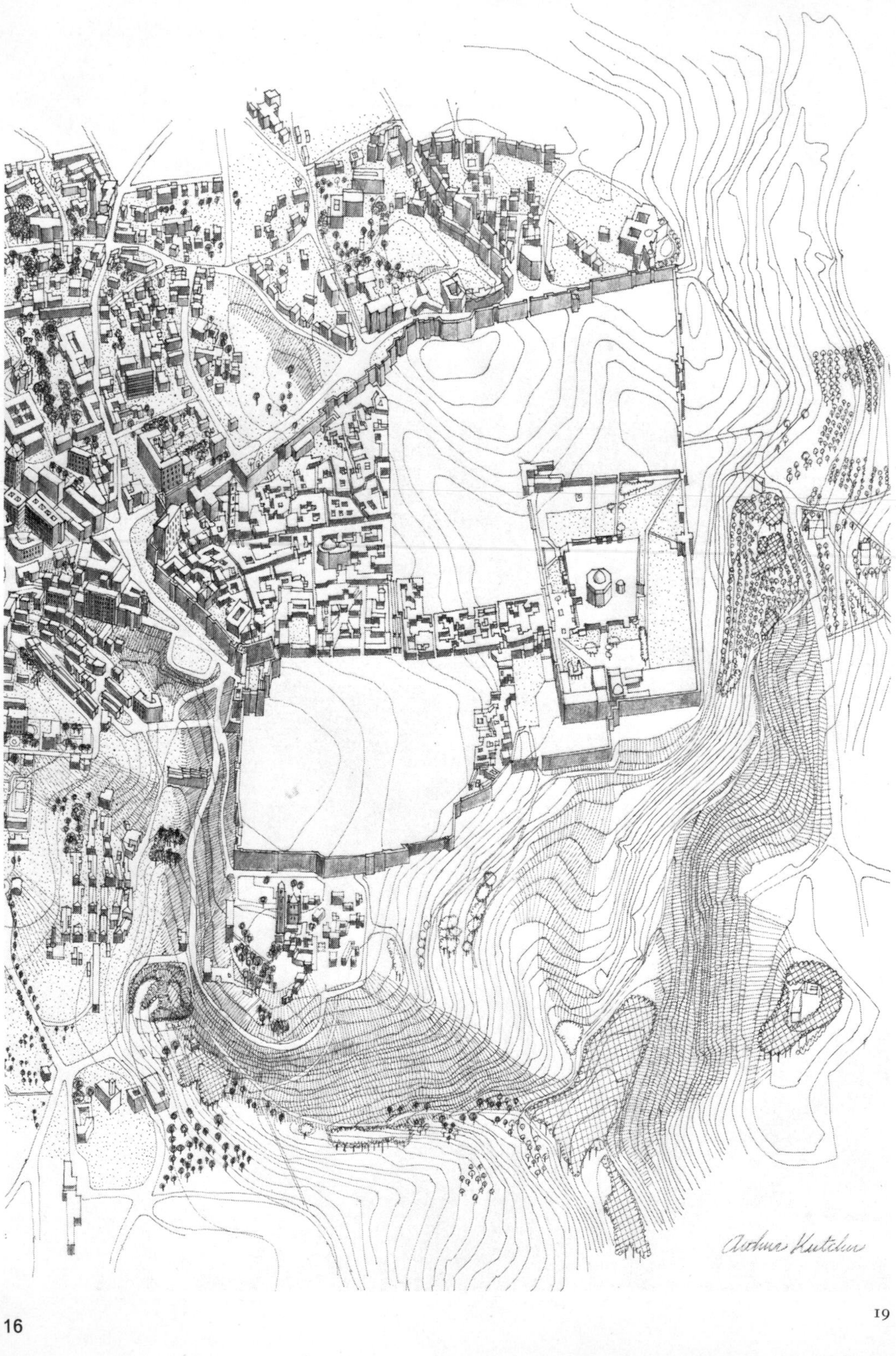
Arthur Kutcher

19

The two monumental features of Jerusalem's built landscape, the Turkish Old City wall and the Temple Mount, built on Herodian foundations, take their placement, their scale, and their details from the physical givens of the site. The wall surrounding the Old City, built in its present form by Suliman the Magnificent in the sixteenth century, an excellent work of military engineering, is also surely an architectural masterpiece. Exemplary by any standards, it is a work that knows not only what it is for, but also precisely where it is. As a fortification it is obviously designed with sight lines and slopes as governing conditions. Yet it follows the line of the hills gracefully, its precise geometry clarifying, rather than overpowering the topography. Seen from the various approaches to the city, the details of the wall's form take into account the path and position of the sun during the course of the day, and the consequent silhouettes and patterns of light and shade created by its crenellation, its towers and turrets. The northern wall's central feature is the Damascus Gate, crowned by an intricate series of decorative pinnacles, designed to be seen from the northern approach to the city, silhouetted against the bright sky, with the Dome of the Rock behind it in the distance. The western city wall, with its regular procession of closely spaced towers, and the Jaffa Gate and Citadel, with their projections, recessions, and prismatic, almost machine-like, modelling and detail, are intended to be seen in angled southern and western sunlight, creating a crisp, rhythmic pattern of light and shade. The southern wall is seen, in conjunction with the Temple Mount, from great distances. It lacks the rich sculptural effects and details of the northern and western walls. The wall becomes severely plain and completely straight as it approaches the Temple

19 Isometric view of the Old City and its immediate surroundings. Portions of the Old City's built areas have been omitted to show the topography within the walls.

20 Aerial view of the Temple Mount and the dense fabric of the city which adjoins it.

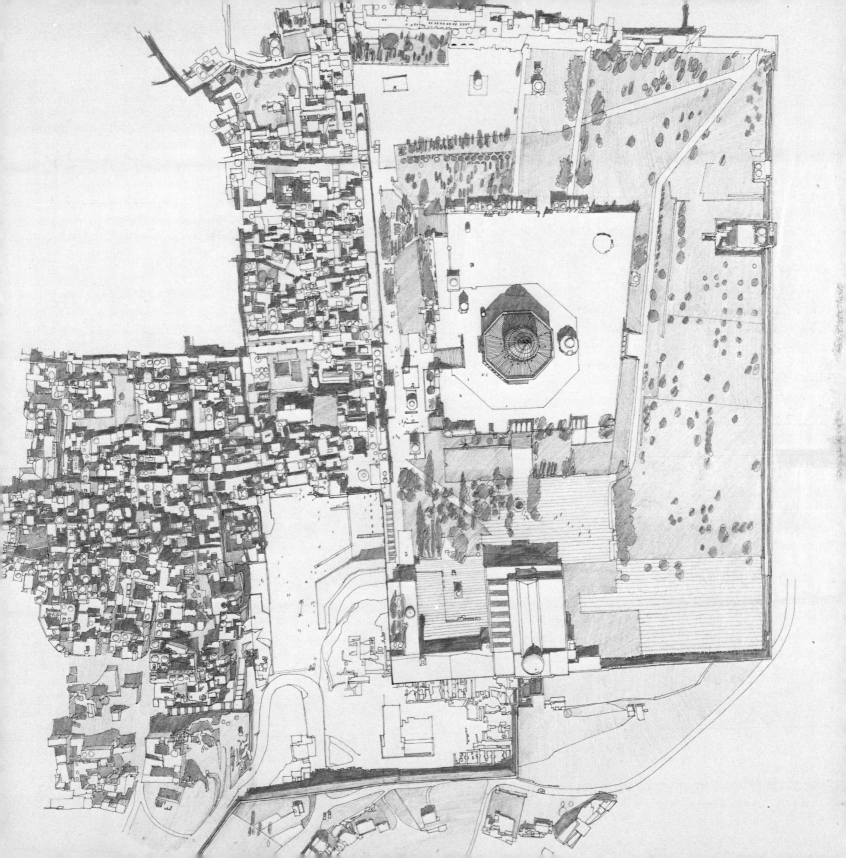

Mount. The eastern city wall is for five hundred metres of its length also the outer retaining wall of the Temple Mount. Except for the Golden Gate, the traditional Messiah's Gate, the wall is straight and unpunctuated, subservient to the great buildings enclosed within and above it.

The Temple Mount, also known as the Noble Sanctuary (Haram al-Sharif) location of the Dome of the Rock and the El Aqsa Mosque, is sited exactly on the foundations of the temple enclosure built by Herod, replacing the temple precinct originally built by King Solomon.

The Temple Mount, a great, nearly rectangular platform measuring some three hundred by five hundred metres, bounded by massive retaining walls, occupies the summit of Mount Moriah, whose slopes fall steeply toward the valley of Jehosaphat on the east and to Kidron on the south. A third valley, the Tyropean on the west, is now mostly filled-in and built upon. Surmounted by the golden

Dome of the Rock, built on the assumed site of Solomon's and later Herod's Temple, this massive artificial hill-top is the most uncompromising, abstractly geometric element in the built landscape of the Old City. It contrasts sharply with the dense, organic fabric of the city which joins it on its northern and western sides, and with the undulating forms of the landscape, bounding it on the east and south. And yet the principles of organization which have formed the Temple Mount are totally interlocked with the structure and rhythms of the landscape which encloses it. Entering the precinct of the Noble Sanctuary from the city's narrow streets, one emerges from the densely packed, bewildering variety and cacophony of the bazaar on to a vast, quiet platform whose visual limits are the ring of hills which surround the Old City: Mt Scopus, the Mount of Olives, the Mount of Offence, and the Mount of Evil Counsel. One sees and senses in an immediate and in a completely physical way the dialectical unity of the place: the overwhelming sky, the

21  The Old City's eastern wall is subservient to the Golden Gate and the Dome of the Rock.

22  The articulations of the Old City's west wall create a strong pattern of shadows. This view from Omaria has been taken over by a block of luxury flats.

22

dazzling crystal clarity of the architecture, the sensuous lines of the distant hills. Then, having ascended the inner platform of the Dome of the Rock, and having walked around it and seen it against its background of hills, one senses it, poised at the centre of the great space enclosing the Old City. Looking westward, the Mosque appears against the background of the 'inner skyline' of the Old City, hundreds of clustered domes punctuated by delicate spires. 'Here everything seems to conspire – nature, the work of man, to produce joy and serenity.'

Nearly everyone senses the serenity of the Haram al-Sharif, the Temple Mount. Perhaps this can be explained in a conceptual way in terms of the centrality, axiality, and symmetry of the Temple Mount in relation to the hills bounding its visual space.

Viewed from the Temple Mount itself, the axial relation between the Dome of the Rock and the El Aqsa Mosque is immediately apparent. The more subtle, but no less powerful visual axes which bind the Temple Mount and its buildings to the surrounding hills can be clearly seen from the platform of the Dome of the Rock. Each of the eight stairways ascending to the platform upon which the Mosque stands is marked at its head by a free-standing arched gateway. There are three gateways on the west, two each on the north and south, and one on the east. All of the gates were built in the fourteenth century, some six hundred years after the Mosque itself. One of the small, three-arched northern gates, and the great, five-arched eastern gate, are precisely aligned with the cardinal axes of the Mosque. Other gates are shifted slightly off their respective

23 The sculptural modelling of the Jaffa Gate and the Citadel.

24 The 'inner skyline' of the Old City as seen from the platform of the Dome of the Rock.

25 The Temple Mount from the air.

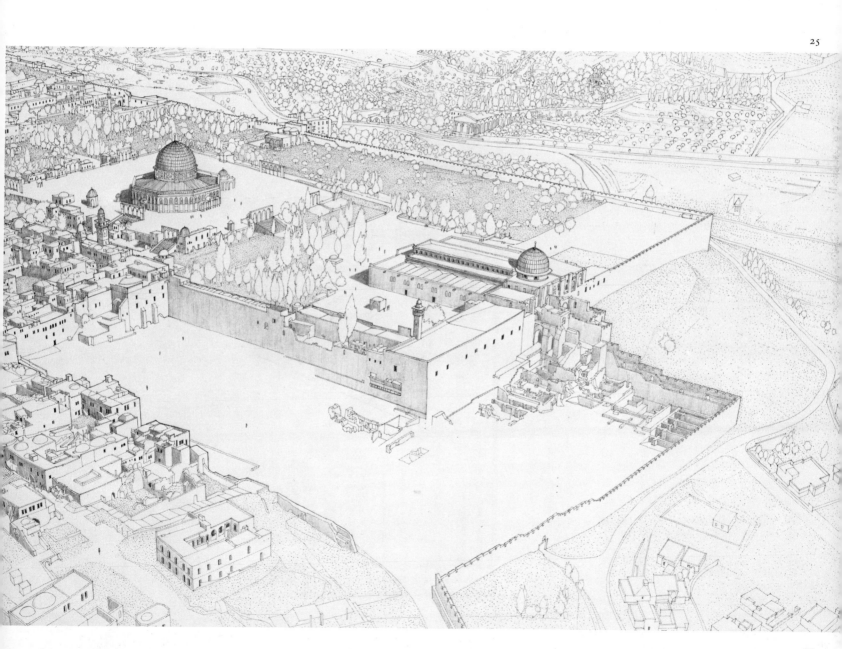

26

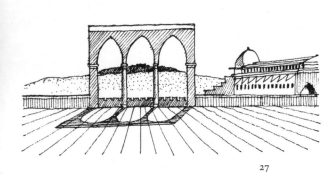

27

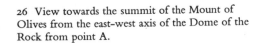

26 View towards the summit of the Mount of Olives from the east-west axis of the Dome of the Rock from point A.

27 Looking south from point A, the Mount of Evil Counsel appears framed in the central portal of the arched gate.

28 Plan of the Temple Mount.

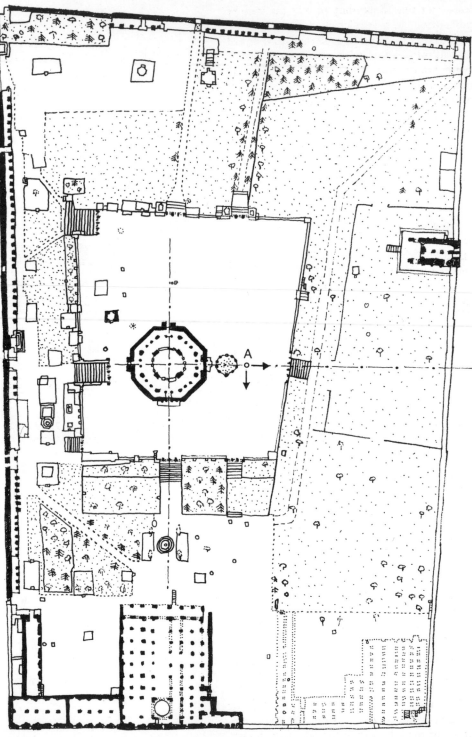

28

axes, and this slight shift of axis, as will be pointed out in a later chapter, is basic to the architectural organization of the Mosque and its platform. The eastern gate marks what is symbolically and aesthetically, though not functionally, the principal approach to the Mosque, the 'Messiah's approach'. Seen from the Mosque's east-west axis, the summit of the Mount of Olives, which is marked by the nineteenth-century Russian bell-tower of Etur, is framed precisely in the centre of the gateway's middle arch. When we realize that this axis also points to the slightly lower thirteenth-century church of the Ascension, traditionally the site of Jesus' ascension to heaven, and that, according to Jewish belief, the Messiah will come to Jerusalem from the east, over the top of the Mount of Olives, we begin to see that a dialogue has taken place over the course of many centuries, a dialogue expressed in the monuments of the great world religions for which Jerusalem is a holy site, and that through this dialogue certain relations and concepts implicit in the siting of the Dome of the Rock, and before it in the siting of the Jewish Temple, have been explicitly and visually expressed.

The recognition of a common theme and its elaboration over the course of history by differing religions and cultures is seen in its full impact from the hills which surround Jerusalem's Old City. Seen from the hills, the bowl-like form of the space which surrounds the Old City is readily apparent, as is the centrality of the Temple Mount within it. Standing on the Mount of Evil Counsel, or on the Mount of Olives, the anchoring points of the cardinal axes of the Dome of the Rock, one is arrested by the power of these axes, and by the sense of equilibrium which the view conveys. Contributing to this sense are the relations of dominance and sub-dominance which obtain between the Temple Mount, the surrounding hills, and the built landscape.

The area's geological structure has produced a rhythm of hill-tops spaced at about eight hundred metre intervals. Mount Moriah, the lowest of the hills within the Old City bowl, sits mid-way between Mount Zion and the

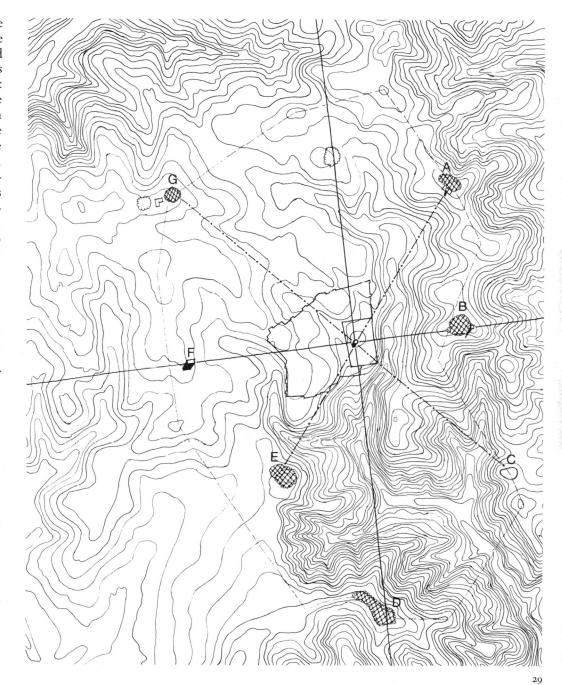

29

29 Map showing the axes of the Dome of the Rock in relation to the key hill-tops in the Old City's visual space. A Mount Scopus; B The Mount of Olives; C Abu-Dis hill; D The Mount of Evil Counsel; E Abu-Tor; F The Plaza Hotel; G Schneller.

33

30

30 Axial view to the Dome of the Rock from the Mount of Olives.

31 Southern elevation of the Temple Mount.

32 Axial view from the Mount of Evil Counsel.

33 The dominant and subdominant elements of the Old City's skyline seen from the Mount of Offence.

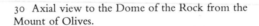

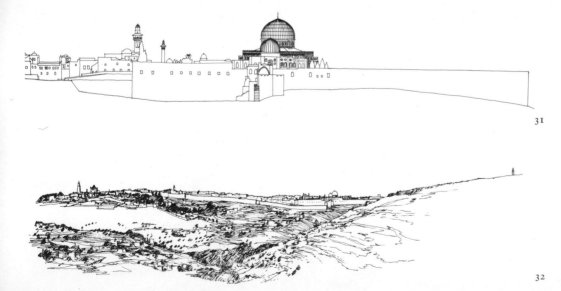

31

32

Mount of Olives and seen from its north-south axis on the Mount of Evil Counsel, the Temple Mount appears framed symmetrically by the two higher hills. Although it is the lowest hill, the Temple Mount, with its axially aligned golden and silver domes, visually dominates the entire space of the Old City. The symmetry and dominance have been heightened by the addition in the nineteenth century of subdominant elements, the delicate vertical accents of the Dormition Tower on Mount Zion and the Russian tower of Etur on the Mount of Olives.

Other hill-tops in this rhythmic sequence lie on the diagonal axis of the octagonal Dome of the Rock, and are also symmetrically disposed upon it. The hill of Abu-Tor and the summit of Mount Scopus each lie sixteen hundred metres from the Mosque, at opposite ends of one of its diagonal axes. The Abu-Tor hill, zoned as public open space but now threatened by speculative development, was an important Byzantine site even before the building of the Mosque, and has been crowned with a fine grove of pine, in the best spirit of the Jerusalem landscape. Thirteen hundred years after the Abu-Tor hill was articulated, the other end of the axis was chosen for the site of the Hebrew University on Mount Scopus (the Mount of Views) by Sir Patrick Geddes, one of the first British mandatory planners. In the thirties, Erich Mendelsohn completed the axis by crowning a fine group of university buildings with his domed library, accentuating the hill-top as another in the series of subdominant

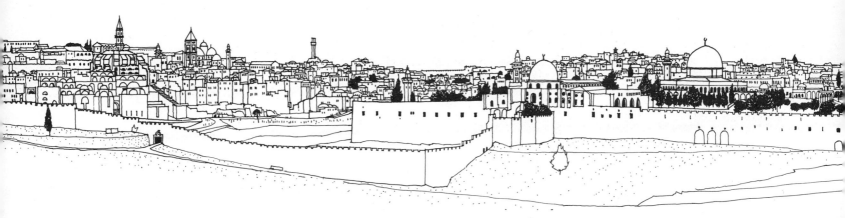

elements which surround the Temple Mount.

The cardinal axes from the Temple to the Mount of Olives and the Mount of Evil Counsel were consciously developed in the design of the Dome of the Rock; these axes were based on relationships which, as we shall later see, were central to the siting of the Temple. The relation of the diagonal axes to their respective hill-tops may not have been consciously realized by the architects of the Mosque, but they were implicit in the design, and have been worked out since.

The most important point, however, is not that these axial relations were always consciously recognized, but that they grow out of the inherent rhythms of the site, and that the Temple Mount, as their focal point, is the place where all the 'visual lines of force' of the landscape come to rest. This equilibrium is seen and felt not only when viewing the Temple Mount from its hill-top axes, but also as the cumulative impression gained by moving around and through the visual space of the Old City, seeing and recalling the changing constellations of minarets, spires and domes, sometimes, because of the clear air, in surprising, even bewildering juxtaposition, always revolving about and subservient to the great golden dome.

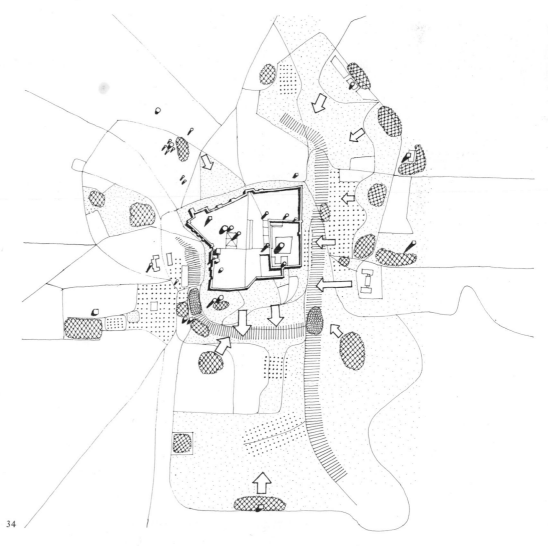

34 The key viewpoints around the Old City. Manmade features, the masses of planting and the dominant domes and spires punctuate the rhythms of the topography to form the area's visual structure. 34

There is an apparent grandeur of scale to the visual basin of the Old City; it often appears to be vast. Because Jerusalem's architecture expresses simple volumes, with minimal window openings, and because structure is not articulated, it is often difficult to judge the actual size of buildings. This contributes to the illusion of vastness, and conversely produces the effect of the compression of distances, like that of the view from King George Street on the western rim of the Old City's visual bowl, from which the Mount of Olives on the eastern rim of the bowl actually appears to be just behind and above the buildings in the foregrounds, with no hint of the nearly two miles of space, containing the old city and its surrounding valleys, which separate them. The ambiguity of this view has been recently resolved in a decisive way by the Ministries of Tourism and Finance and the Jerusalem Municipality, by blocking it with a giant luxury hotel.

The visual area of the Old City is in fact quite small, about two by three miles from horizon to horizon; its dominant buildings, by the standards of Western architecture, are miniatures. The delicacy of its landscape and of its buildings would be crushed by the presence of ordinary, medium sized contemporary buildings and roads, and the ambiguity and impressiveness of its scale would be erased.

A comparison of the visual structure and size of Jerusalem's Old City area with those of other famous cities should make this apparent.

35 This view from King George V Street in west
Jerusalem to the Mount of Olives beyond the Old
City has been obliterated by a giant luxury apartment
hotel, The Plaza.

36 View from the Pincio Gardens to St Peter's on the skyline of Rome.

37 A medieval view of the cathedral in Florence from across the Arno.

36

London, Florence and Rome all are marked by religious monuments which have traditionally dominated their respective skylines, each in a different way. London's St Paul's Cathedral, originally designed by Sir Christopher Wren as the culmination of a series of Baroque street vistas, dominated the city, even though Wren's Baroque town-planning scheme was never carried out. Seen from along, on, and across London's great visual space, the Thames, the magnificent dome rode high above the city's lesser buildings and spires. The uncompromising nature of this panorama began to be eroded with the intense development of London's city as a centre of banking and

38 An eighteenth century view of St Paul's in London from Southwark.

39 The Dome of the Rock and the Mount of Olives behind it from the roof of the Petra Hotel.

37

28

40 The Dome of the Rock is seen from within the Area A.

41 The Cathedral in Florence dominates axial vistas from within the city as well as from the surrounding hills.

42 St Peter's in Rome and the hill-top views to it.

43 The visual space of St Paul's in London is the Thames and its environs.

44 View from Mount Scopus.

44

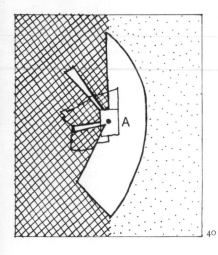

40

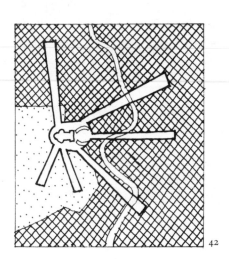

42

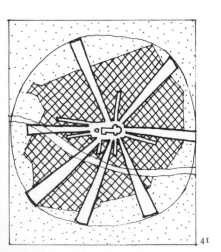

41

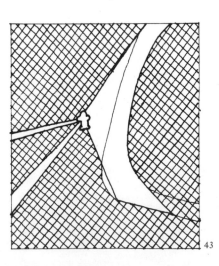

43

commerce in the nineteenth century. And now the Greater London Council with its 'high building policy' has accomplished what even the Luftwaffe failed to do: it has blotted out St Paul's.

The Dome of the cathedral in Florence, generally considered the first great work of the Italian Renaissance, is the strongest element on the city's skyline as seen from the surrounding hills. It also dominates the visual structure of Florence in another, more important way. The dome rises directly from the octagon of the Gothic east end of the cathedral, so that its full height can be appreciated from close as well as distant views. The cathedral's piazza is a focal point in the street pattern of Medieval and Renaissance Florence, allowing the dome to be seen or glimpsed in its full height from many points within the fabric of the city, creating a cumulative impression of its dominance. Unlike Florence Cathedral, St Peter's Basilica at the Vatican was built outside the city of Rome. Its scale therefore had to be sufficient to dominate distant views from the city itself, and today, seen from Rome's hills – the Aventine, the Palatine, Monte Mario – and from the Pincio and the Quirinale, St Peter's does act as a solid visual anchor and indisputably rules over the many lesser domes on Rome's skyline. These distant views at roof-top level are the only ones which reveal the Basilica's true form. Closer views from Bernini's

45 The Dome of the Rock appears on the skyline seen from the lower slope of the Mount of Olives.

46 The Dome with Mount Scopus behind it seen from mid-slope on the Abu-Tor Hill.

47 The Dome of the Rock against the backdrop of the Old City viewed from the Mount of Olives.

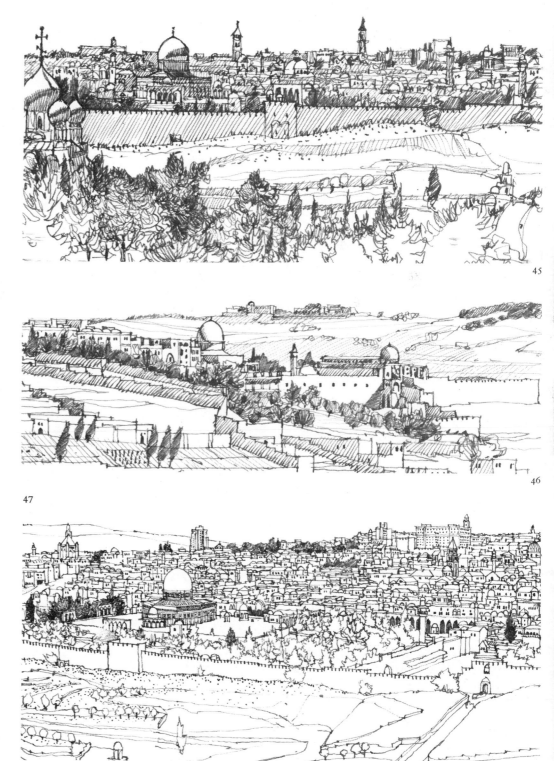

45

46

47

Piazza immediately in front of St Peter's give no adequate impression of the height and scale of Michelangelo's dome, since the nave and portico added later by Carlo Maderna block its view. Fortunately for Rome and Florence, the planning authorities consider the visual structure of their cities as part of their cultural heritage, and stringent height limits protect the character of both cities' skylines.

The Temple Mount's special kind of dominance within its visual basin is similar in some respects to the characteristics of each of the three other cities. Like London's St Paul's, the Temple Mount's visual domain is not limited to a few hill-top and street vistas, but consists of a great sweep of space. Like the cathedral in Florence, the Dome of the Rock sits within a bowl of hills, lying however not in the city's heart, but at its edge, as does St Peter's in Rome. But in three important ways the relation of the Temple Mount to its surroundings is unique. First of all, the Temple Mount is, with the exception of the Wailing Wall compound, the lowest part of the Old City, and its buildings are therefore hardly seen from within the city walls, or from the new city on higher ground to the west. Secondly, although the Dome of the Rock sometimes appears on the skyline when seen from the valleys below it, or from mid-slope on the surrounding hills, when viewed from the tops of these hills, because Mount Moriah is the lowest of them,

48

49

the dome always appears against the backdrop of the landscape, below either the skyline of the surrounding hills, or that of the city to the west.

The third factor which makes the Old City's visual quality unique is its scale. The Old City's basin is considerably smaller than the heart of London, or of Rome; and the Old City itself would fit neatly into a corner of Hyde Park, or into the grounds of the Villa Borghese in Rome, with plenty of room to spare. Because of the area's small scale, the

views within it are such that the relation of the Old City to its setting can be clearly grasped in a single glance from a relatively short distance, with landmarks easily recognizable.

It has already been pointed out that the siting of the Temple Mount is based upon the principle of the equilibrium of the total landscape at a single point. Its finely balanced position, together with its relatively low site and small scale, make the dominance of the Dome of the Rock within its visual space extremely delicate, much more susceptible to

the threat of massive tower blocks and high-rise slabs, than are the monuments of Rome, Florence, or London, where the need for height control has long been recognized, if not always respected.

But in Jerusalem, there is no official high building policy, nor any limit to the height of buildings. What is more, without reference to any guide lines whatsoever, a massive slug of high-rise projects have already been approved. How this came about, and what can be done about it, is the subject of a later chapter.

48  Map of the central area of Jerusalem.

49  Map of central London to the same scale.
A  Regent's Park; B  Hyde Park; C  Imperial
College.

50  Elevation of the Dome of the Rock.

51  Elevation of St Paul's Cathedral in London to
the same scale.

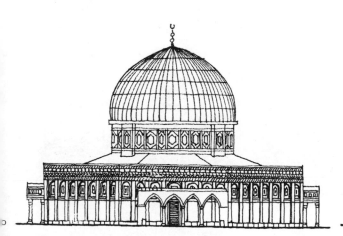

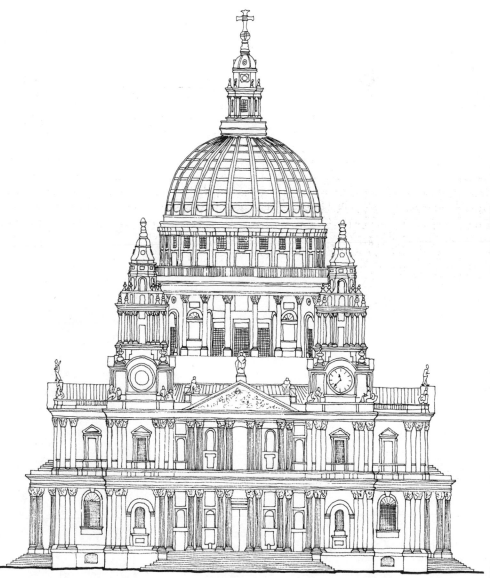

SENATVS
POPVLVSQVEROMANVS
DIVOTITO·DIVIVESPASIANIF
VESPASIANO·AVGVSTO

52  The Arch of Titus in Rome, commemorating
the capture and destruction of Jerusalem by the
Tenth Legion.

34

# II The site and its symbols: images from the past

*'Walk about Zion, and go round about her: count the towers thereof*

*Mark ye well her bulwarks, consider her palaces; that ye may tell it to the generation following'*

AS WE HAVE SEEN, the Old City is in some of its basic features a typical example of Roman imperial town-planning. In the plan of the walls, a square which has been bent to follow the topography, and the cross axis of its *cardo* and *decumanus*, it typifies the Roman colonial town. The Temple Mount even has a Roman parallel in the Capitol built in 42 BC upon the ruins of Carthage, destroyed as was Herod's Jerusalem, by the Roman legions. Hill-top platforms are, however, not typical of Roman construction.

In its most important aspects the Temple Mount embodies a unique synthesis of Mediterranean and Mesopotamian themes: its rational geometry relates not only building to building as in the west, but the entire complex to the surrounding landscape. The holy mountain as an artificially-raised platform is a common feature of several ancient Mesopotamian temple sites. These artificial mounds, such as those at Uruk and at the Temple of Ishtar-Kititum at Ishchali, of the third and second millennia BC, were set in the flat Mesopotamian landscape, dominating the countryside for great distances, and raising the god's house closer to heaven. The platform itself was usually not a simple rectangle, and the cultic buildings upon it were related to each other by a kind of organic interlocking of forms, rather than by axial alignment.

Axial siting principles were developed in the Mediterranean basin. Egyptian funerary temples, such as the great complex of Amun at Karnak of the second millennium BC, were built symmetrically about a single processional axis. The use of the cross axis seems to trace its origins to Asia Minor where it was first used by the Ionians. Later Greeks developed it as the expression of a rational ideal, as did the Romans, who made it the symbol of their town-planning. In addition to forming the basis for colonial settlements, the cross axis was used by the Romans in an architectural way to link together hierarchically organized, internally consistent spatial complexes, exemplified in the Roman Forums. Groups of buildings and the spaces between them formed self-contained, axially arranged units which were in turn tied to adjacent complexes by the crossing at key points of their respective axes. The cross axis as an organizing principle which generated a vast sequence of built and open spaces was fully exploited at Hadrian's Villa, near Rome.

In the Semitic East, groupings of sacred buildings were usually not linked together axially in this way. Instead, individual monuments acted as solids, marking key points within the large space of the landscape, activating this space and giving it a specific scale. The fundamental motive of this kind of siting was not to impose a man-made order upon nature: rather, by the sensitive placement of sympathetically scaled, clearly man-made forms within the landscape it created a spatial dialogue between the two. In Palestine, unlike Mesopotamia, there was no attempt to raise the god's house above its surroundings. Cultic shrines were seldom sited on the highest hills, which were considered too wind-swept and exposed for either living or worship. The

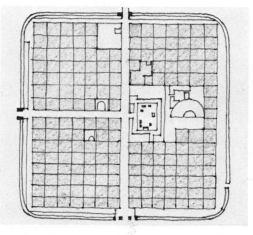

53 Plan of Timgad, a Roman colonial town of the first century A.D.

54 Plan of Aelia Capitolina built over the ruins of Herod's Jerusalem.

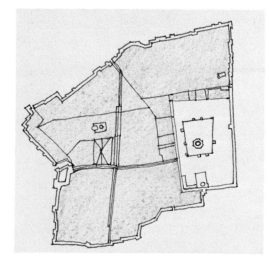

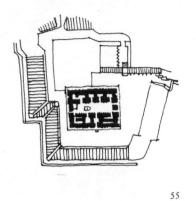

55

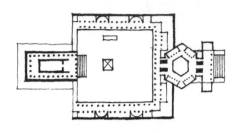

57

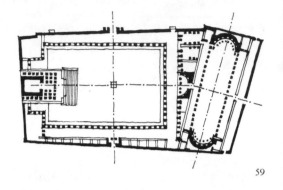

59

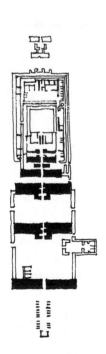

56

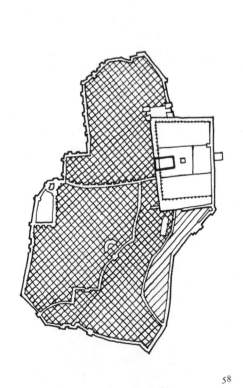

58

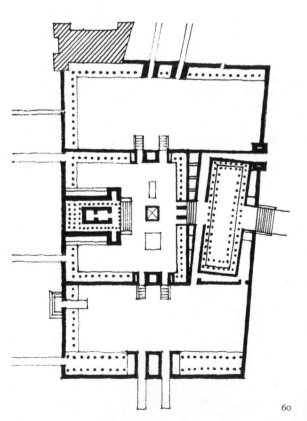

60

61

sacred groves of the fertility cults were often in valleys, and cultic mounds were usually lower than the surrounding hills.

At the Temple Mount of Jerusalem's Old City, these sets of contrasting architectural principles come together in a special way. The Mesopotamian theme of an artificial temple platform has been imposed upon an existing Judean hill-top in a thoroughly Roman manner. It is an essay in Roman engineering skill with the textbook clarity of its geometry, its brilliant technique, and its massive construction. The buildings upon the Temple Mount, though cited according to the Roman cross axis, do not join together to form a self-contained spatial complex. They define focal points within the much larger space of the bowl of hills surrounding the Old City. The cross axes themselves are not arbitrarily imposed, in the Roman manner. They derive their alignment from the major features of the landscape, and they determine in a very un-Roman way, 'from the outside in', the position and the relation between the buildings of the Temple Mount. (It should be noted that the Herodian design for the Temple Mount may have attempted to create an enclosed Roman forum on the site of what had previously been, without doubt, a hill-top platform. In any event, Herod's Temple only stood for thirty years before being destroyed by the Tenth Legion, and if it bore a resemblance to the many conjectural representations of it, then it must have been ponderous and inappropriate to the site.)

The Dome of the Rock itself gives the most direct and most striking expression to the union of opposites, the balance of the rational and the sensual, which has formed the entire Temple Mount. The geometrical conception and structural execution of the Mosque are drawn from the Mediterranean world. Its harmonious, mathematically derived proportions are Greek. The structural concept of the dome was inherited from Imperial Rome by Byzantium, which developed the concept into the characteristic feature of its architecture. But if the Mosque's geometric clarity and structural logic are Western, the immediate

55 Plan of the Temple Platform at Uruk in Mesopotamia, third millennium B C.

56 Temple complex at Karnak, second millennium B C.

57 The Temple of Jupiter at Baalbek, first century A D.

58 Herodian Jerusalem.

59 Forum of Leptis Magna, third century A D.

60 The Herodian Temple Mount, first century A D.

61 Funerary towers near Palmyra.

sensuous impact of the dazzling coloured patterns of its glazed-tile sheathing certainly comes from the East. Similar use was made of coloured ceramic facing for sacred structures throughout ancient Mesopotamia for thousands of years. In these ways man-made Jerusalem incorporates in built form an interlocking of opposites which recalls that found in her landscape, her climate, and in her soils. The synthesis of Eastern and Western themes of sacred architecture does not completely explain the fascination which the site held for both the ancient East and West. It merely records a process by which each culture adopted and transformed, in its own way, elements which were traditional to the other, and by developing in time it has made visually explicit certain implicit physical qualities of the site. It was the awareness of these implicit qualities, an awareness shared by both cultures, which generated the long process.

The feeling shared over thousands of years that Jerusalem is a sacred site comes, then, not only from the religiously significant events which have occurred there, but also from the fundamental physical nature of the place. To the ancient Hebrews particularly, the site must have seemed an appropriate place to worship and communicate with a deity who was both immanent and transcendent, a deity with whom men could speak. The site does not present infinite perspectives. Its limited vistas, its sense of definition and enclosure tie the place to the earth. The shrines and altars are not arrogantly above, they are part of and within the tangible world. On the other hand only a place which physically embodied perfection was suitable as the site of God's House, and in that respect as well Mount Moriah, central and serene in the landscape, was ideal. It should be noted in this connection that to the ancient Canaanites and Hebrews, the present state of the Old City area, with its hill-tops articulated by groves and by towers, would be for philosophical reasons unthinkable. These are nineteenth century additions, and they are all Northern European, but fortunately they did the wrong thing in the right way. The delicacy of their scale and the sensitivity of their placement are wholly within

62

62 Interior view of the Dome of the Rock.

63 Decorative tiles.

64 View of the Dome of the Rock.

the local tradition of point markers which enter into a dialogue with the landscape. With these recent additions, the implicit visual energies of the Old City's landscape have been worked out to their completion.

There is another phenomenon which may help to explain the tremendous power which the site exerted upon the mind of ancient man. A common feature of the solar cults of the ancient Middle East was the siting of shrines on an axis defined by the rising and setting of the sun on the autumnal equinox. The Temple of Jupiter at Baalbek (the ancient Heliopolis) is an example of this kind of siting. On the Temple Mount in Jerusalem the east-west axis of the Dome of the Rock, and undoubtedly of both

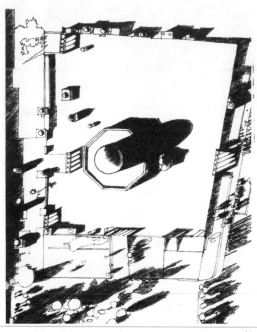

65 View to Theodosius from Mount Zion. The visual forces of the Old City's landscape have been worked out to completion.

66 Aerial view of the Dome of the Rock and its platform.

65

Jewish temples before it, is defined as at Baalbek by the path of the equinoctial sun. That the solar principle was basic both to the siting of the temple and also to some of the rites performed there is evidenced by the prophet Ezekiel's condemnation of these rites as the greatest of the abominations committed at the Temple. 'Hast thou seen *this*, O son of man? Turn thee yet again and thou shalt see greater abominations than these. And he brought me into the inner court of the Lord's house, and behold, at the door of the Temple of the Lord, between the porch and the altar, were about five and twenty men with their backs toward the temple of the Lord, and their faces toward the east, and they worshipped the sun toward the east.' Ez. 8, 15–16. This solar phenomenon can be observed today.

From a position on the east-west axis in front of the Mosque, the equinoctial sun appears to rise over the summit of the Mount of Olives. Viewed from the axis on the Mount of Olives, the sun appears to set behind the Dome of the Rock.

It was this astronomical phenomenon combined with the qualities of the landscape which must have given the site its apparently cosmic significance: for here was the harmonious union of the most powerful of dualities, expressed in the clearest possible way. The site of the sacred building was the place where the respective equilibriums of heaven and earth coincided, and this intersection was made explicit through the rational ideal of the cross axis. In the design and siting of the Dome of the Rock and the El Aqsa Mosque, these

conceptual relationships find their complete physical fulfilment.

The theme of the cross axis seems to be intimately tied with Jerusalem in a symbolic as well as a visual way. Erich Neumann summarizes the history of this symbol. 'The symbol of the circular mandala stands at the beginning as at the end. In the beginning it takes the mythological form of Paradise, in the end of Heavenly Jerusalem. The perfect figure of the circle from whose centre radiate the four arms of the cross, in which the opposites are at rest is a very early and a very late symbol historically. It is found in the sanctuaries of the Stone Age, it is the Paradise where the four streams have their source, and in Canaanite mythology it is the Central Point where the Great God El (Hebrew: Elohim) sits, at the

67

67 Plan of the Solar axis from the Mount of Olives to the Dome of the Rock (defined by the rising and setting of the equinoctic sun), and its perpendicular axis to the Mount of Evil Counsel.

68 Above, the circular mandala; below, a section taken from the survey done by Captain Charles Warren RE, 1867.

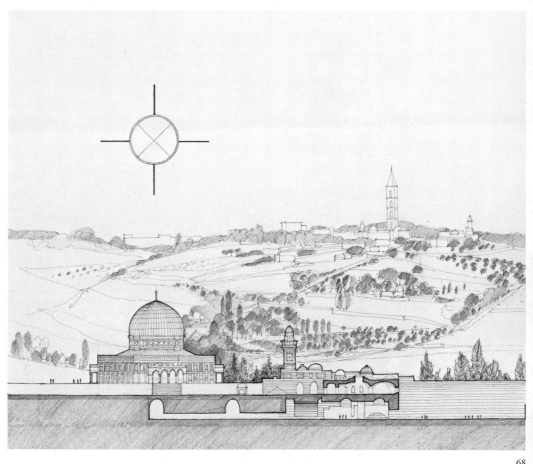

68

source of the streams in the midst of the two seas.' In this central and serene place all the forces of heaven and earth come together at rest; yet the site is poised on the knife edge between two worlds. The landscape of which it is the centre is in a state of swift transition. Within the distance of a single mile it changes from one world into another, from the congenial Mediterranean region to the harsh and hostile desert. That deep tensions underlie the placid balance finds expression in myths and legends about the sacred site, as well as in its fearful history. The Rock of Abraham, site of the sacrifice, and later of Mohammed's night journey to Heaven, is the legendary centre of the world. Beneath it the four rivers of paradise have their source, and there also the souls of all mankind await redemption.

But also according to legend common to Jews and Muslims, the sacred rock, the centre of the earth, is poised over the bottomless abyss of endless chaos.

These legends have their ultimate source in ancient mythologies, but they can also be related to feelings which come out of the confrontation with the visual and physical qualities of the site.

To devout Jews, Muslims, and Christians, the visual character and beauty of the site have another kind of spiritual dimension. The city and its landscape take on an associative and symbolic meaning because of what has happened there, or in other words, the present reality is elevated because of its past. The Jerusalem of the present, the hills and valleys, the rocks and the trees, the walls and buildings

are all in a way the residue of a sacred past. For Jews, specifically, Jerusalem has also meant the future, the hope and promise of homecoming and of redemption, while for Christians Jerusalem has come to mean the Heavenly Jerusalem of St John's Revelation, the symbol of the joy and perfection of another world. Somehow, with the city as the centre for all these symbolic and spiritual concerns, the real and present Jerusalem has suffered. Mole-like the devout scour the site for sacred relics, never sensing Jerusalem's natural grandeur; religious thrill-seekers in search of the occult never notice the organic unity and completeness of city and landscape which is the source of her sacredness, and all the while, watching this process very closely, hand on the bulldozer throttle, are the developers, waiting for their chance.

41

69

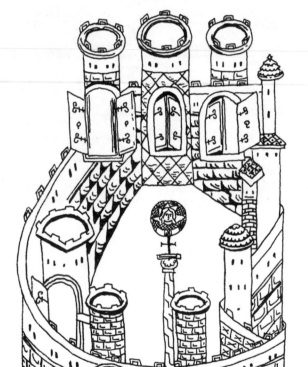

70

## Pictorial Representations and Plans

The representations of Jerusalem in drawings and plans from the past show that the present narrowness of vision amongst the religious is a recent phenomenon. Almost all have one feature in common; they treat the city as an organic whole and as part of a larger perceptual unity. The relation between the city and the landscape is usually as important as the internal structure of the city itself. None of these drawings, including the author's own, communicate the true visual sense of the place; that sense eludes all forms of pictorial representation, including photography, and in a curious way often seems to come through most vividly in the most abstract views. There is also a strong difference in spirit between the work of local residents, and the work of visitors. The latter invariably impose a vision of their native Europe upon the middle-eastern reality. This is particularly striking in medieval views which show a Jerusalem composed of a forest of gothic spires. Views drawn by travellers also seem consistently to repeat certain basic mistakes in the city's form, suggesting that most were done at second hand from supposedly authoritative sources, rather than from the site itself. The views which most successfully capture the visual quality of the city are the nineteenth century Jewish ones, done without the benefit of the science of perspective. Strangely enough, the professional nineteenth century representations, with their proper use of perspective and generally correct proportions, are among the least convincing views. The viewpoints most often used are the famous panoramas, frequently from the Mount of Olives overlooking the city.

69 Detail from the Arch of Titus.

70 A seventh-century view of Jerusalem.

71 A drawing of the Holy Sepulchre, 1362.

72 Jerusalem, from a French fifteenth-century manuscript.

73 Moslem artists did not produce pictorial representations. Shown above are decorative tiles from the Dome of the Rock.

43

74 Italian map, 1588.

75 Drawing found in the itinerary of St Werro, 1581.

76 German view from the Mount of Olives, early eighteenth century.

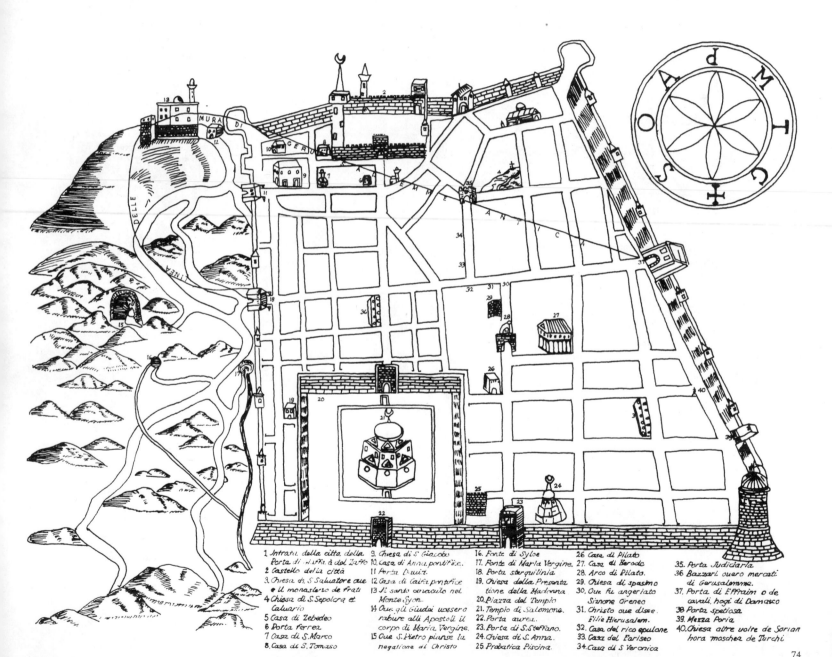

1. Intratta della città della Porta di Hiffa, è del Zaffo
2. Castello della città
3. Chiesa di S. Salvatore oue e il monasterio de frati
4. Chiesa di S. Sepolcra et Caluario
5. Casa di Zebedeo
6. Porta ferrea
7. Casa di S. Marco
8. Casa di S. Tomaso
9. Chiesa di S. Giacobo
10. Casa di Anna pontifice.
11. Porta Duuiz
12. Casa di Caifa pontifice
13. Il santo cenaculo nel Monte Syon.
14. Oue gli Giudai uossero rabure alli Apostoli il corpo di Maria Vergine.
15. Oue S. Pietro piunse la nagatione di Christo
16. Fonte di Syloe
17. Fonte di Maria Vergine
18. Porta sterquilinia
19. Chiesa della Presentatione della Madonna
20. Piazza del Tempio
21. Tempio di Salomone
22. Porta aurea.
23. Porta di S. Steffano
24. Chiesa di S. Anna.
25. Probatica Piscina
26. Casa di Pilato
27. Casa di Erode
28. Arco di Pilato.
29. Chiesa di spasimo
30. Oue fu angeriato Simone Cireneo
31. Christo oue disse Filie Hierusalem.
32. Casa del rico epulone
33. Casa del Fariseo
34. Casa di S. Veronica
35. Porta Judiciaria.
36. Bazzari ouaro mercati di Gerusalemme.
37. Porta di Effraim o de cavali, hogi di Damasco
38. Porta spetiosa
39. Mezza Porta
40. Chiesa altre volte de Sorian hora moschea de Turchi.

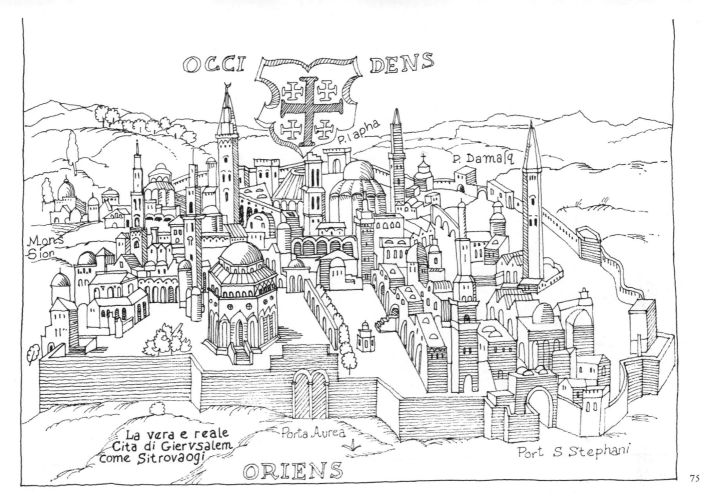

OCCI DENS

P. Iapha

P. Damasq

Mons Sion

La vera e reale
Cita di Giervsalem
come Sitrovaogi

Porta Aurea

Port S Stephani

ORIENS

75

76

77 The Holy Places of Jerusalem, 1850.

78 Jerusalem and its vicinity, 1875.

79 The Wailing Wall and the Temple site drawn by Shemuel Shulman, a native of Jerusalem, 1887.

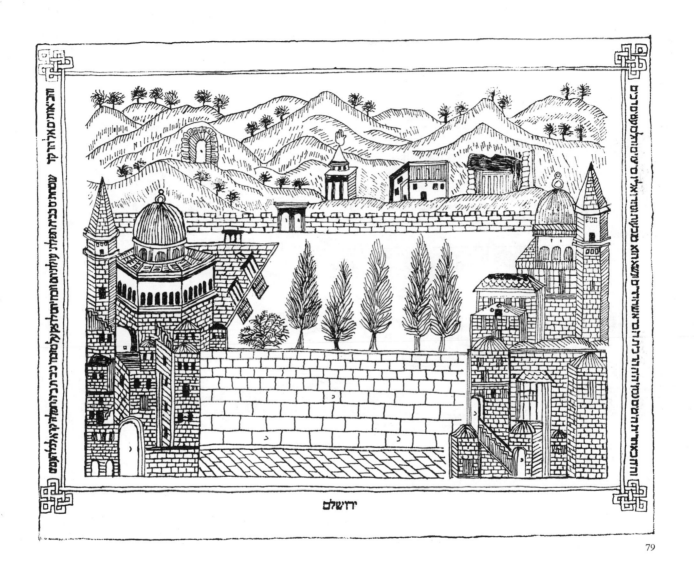

ירושלם

79

80  A view of the Temple Mount and the Mount
of Olives from the Jewish quarter, 1971. ➤

47

The common themes which had guided the ancient, medieval, and nineteenth century builders of Jerusalem, and which have inspired those who depicted the city through its history, were also themes which the town planners of the British Mandatory Government recognized as valid and viable, and became the basis of the mandatory plans for Jerusalem. These themes were later continued and elaborated upon in an exemplary way by Israeli planners during the first decade of the State's existence. It is only in the past few years that other, opposing tendencies have arisen.

The first mandatory town plans were based upon the premise that the Old City and its surrounding landscape constituted an organic unity, and that within this unity, the Holy City itself was to be considered as the physical expression of a spiritual ideal. For this reason, the area was to be protected from the encroachment of urbanization by marking off a large open area, a 'green belt' around the Old City. The major portion of new urban development was to take place to the west of the Old City, on Jerusalem's Mediterranean plateau.

The first mandatory plan by Maclean in 1918 set about realizing these principles by defining an inner and outer ring of protection around the Old City. The inner ring with an average width of about three hundred metres was the 'prohibited zone' within which no buildings were to be allowed. The outer 'restricted zone' was defined as a rough semi circle with an outer boundary between two thousand and three thousand metres from the Temple Mount, comprising the northern two thirds of the Old City's visual basin. There was also a narrower 'restricted zone' on the west of the city. Within this zone, buildings were allowed by special permission only after a detailed architectural review. The rest of the plan showed a compact new city on the west with a roughly radial-concentric road layout.

The 1922 plan by Ashbee and Geddes translated the abstract geometry of Maclean's 'restricted' zone into a realistic boundary based upon existing land ownership and upon the topography. The area was defined as public open space, and it began to connect with other, smaller open spaces to form the beginning of a city-wide system. The plan for the new western position of the city expressed Garden City principles: decentralized work zones were distributed among the residential areas. The plan did not define commercial areas.

The 1934 Holliday plan was the first legal zoning map for the city. The area of open space around the old city was reduced somewhat on its south-west and north-east sides, but it maintained the spirit of the previous plans. An important concept was added within the old city's open space. Recognizing the special character of the old city's landscape, it was declared a nature reserve, rather than a 'green belt' park as in previous plans. The plan provided for a linear commercial centre, along the axis of the Jaffa Road. The plan's road system was based upon topographical realities, and some additional parks were added in the western part of the city.

The Kendall plan of 1944 was the first instance of an unfortunate tendency among Jerusalem town-planners which was later to become a stampede. Kendall's plan as originally proposed, and the studies which backed it up, were an admirable piece of work. Unfortunately, due to political pressures, the open space around the old city was drastically reduced to fifty metre strips on three sides, and commercial development was allowed to encroach upon it, virtually to the Jaffa Gate. No new open spaces were proposed for the western part of the city.

The first Israeli plan for Jerusalem done in 1948 by Rau was a brilliant development of the basic mandatory planning principles. Rau's plan further elaborated concepts derived from Jerusalem's special quality, and his work in this respect still dominates the ideology of Jerusalem planners, if not their practices. Rau proposed a 'green belt' of nature reserve and agricultural land around the entire city. All of the Old City's landscape area was included in this green belt.

A generous public park faced the Old City on its west, and was connected with the rest of the city's open spaces to form a completely interconnected system of parks whose form was derived from the givens of the topography. In the new city's visual basin, a gentler version of the Old City area, Rau proposed a series of roughly Old City-sized nuclear units separated by the system of open spaces. Located in the centre of the new city's visual bowl were the Israeli government centre and the new Hebrew University, on the western mirror-image of the Old City's site. The plan proposed a linear commercial centre which served both the older and newer parts of West Jerusalem. Rau's was the first plan to recognize the need for the preservation of areas built outside the Old City; and several of the older neighbourhoods in Western Jerusalem were included in this category.

The basic concepts which generated the plan were drawn from Jerusalem's physical realities, and from her social traditions. Its scheme of neighbourhood units separated by open spaces (found also in the preliminary version of Kendall's 1944 plan) was derived from the series of more or less ethnically homogeneous community units which had characterized both the old and new cities' physical and social form. The relation of built to open spaces found in the plan was based upon the area's topography, and also upon traditional Jerusalem siting principles: the valleys were green open spaces, the hill slopes received a carpet of housing, and the ridge tops were reserved for public and institutional buildings, all of which expressed in built form the community's scale of values. In this way, themes encountered in the old city and its area were continued in the new city. Thus, Rau's concept of new Jerusalem was open, horizontal, nucleated, introverted and hierarchic.

After the division of the city in 1948, two very different tendencies were encountered in the plans for the eastern and western halves of the city. On the Israeli side of the armistice line, Rau's 1948 plan served as the conceptual basis for the new city's development, while the 1944 Kendall plan with its later amendments outlined the patterns of growth for the Jordanian half of the city, which included most of the Old City area.

The 1956 outline plan by Shviv, which became the city's 1959 legal plan, translated Rau's concept into a statutory zoning map. There were some relatively minor changes in Rau's proposed relation of open spaces and built-up areas for the western basin of the new city, and the open space link between this area and the parks facing the old city was eliminated, but Shviv's plan retained Rau's linear commercial centre, as well as the horizontal and open character of the original concept. The plan prescribed a legal height limit of five storeys, and made provision for preserving the city's major views. The plan's road layout followed the basic radial-concentric network deriving from Holliday's 1934 plan. In the summary by the Ministry of the Interior, under the section on skyline and view presentation, the plan's intent was clearly expressed: 'Noteworthy is the emphasis put on the problem of the skyline and the magnificent panoramas of Jerusalem, which are to be left open and unobstructed.' Although these principles took the form of legal restrictions, that did not prevent the authorities from completely ignoring them in their subsequent planning decisions.

If on the Israeli side of the armistice line wilful and arbitrary decisions by the authorities were eroding the principles of an excellent town plan, on the Jordanian side a series of compromises, forced by political and economic pressures, had resulted in a plan which was a sad parody of the original mandatory idealism. The 1964 Jordanian plan had reduced the Old City's open space to a minimal strip around the city walls, with the adjacent Muslim and Jewish cemeteries added to it. The only other open space within all of the Old City's landscape was proposed for the Hebrew University site on Mount Scopus, which was in any event under Israeli custodianship, and out of the plan's jurisdiction. The rest of the Old City's landscape – hills, slopes, and valleys – was zoned in its entirety for residential development.

All of these town plans recognized and, as far as possible, tried to implement the concepts which were basic to the first mandatory schemes. The failure of some plans to maintain these concepts in the face of pressures for development does not indicate that any new

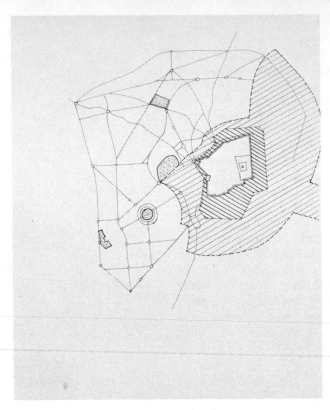

81 The first mandatory plan for Jerusalem by
Maclean, 1918.

83 Holliday's plan, 1934.

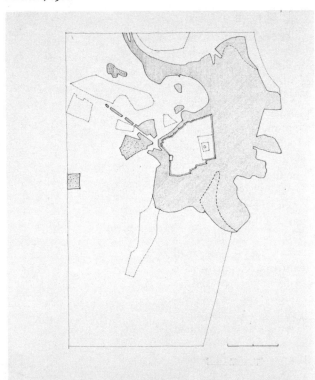

82 Plan by Ashbee and Geddes of 1922.

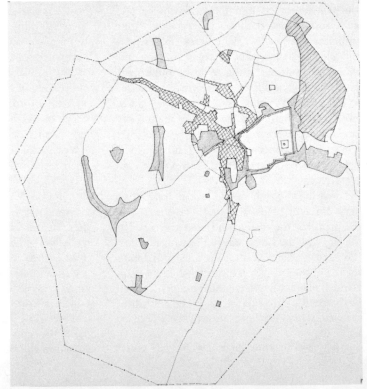

84 The 1944 Kendall plan.

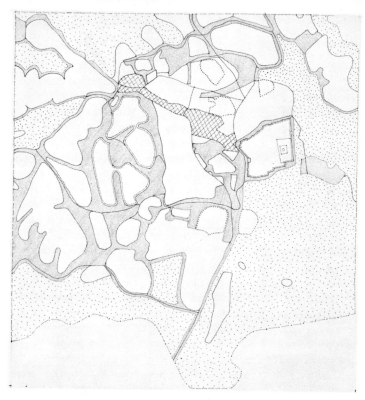

85 Plan by Rau, 1948.

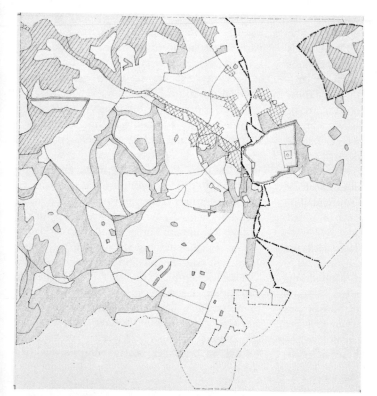

86 The Shviv-Kendall plan, 1956–64.

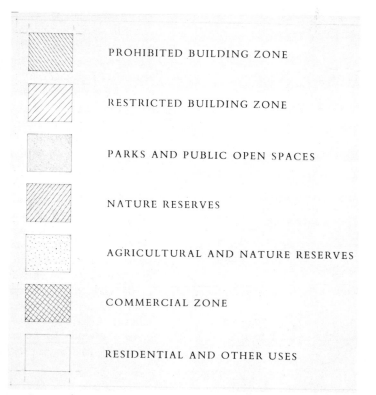

87 The Jerusalem Master Plan 1968 by
Hashimshoni, Schweid, and Hashimshoni.

PROHIBITED BUILDING ZONE

RESTRICTED BUILDING ZONE

PARKS AND PUBLIC OPEN SPACES

NATURE RESERVES

AGRICULTURAL AND NATURE RESERVES

COMMERCIAL ZONE

RESIDENTIAL AND OTHER USES

53

planning ideology had replaced the original principles, but only that the planners had lost the battle to the politicians.

The most recent plan for the city, the Master Plan of 1968 by Hashimshoni, Schweid, and Hashimshoni, has been the centre of a public controversy ever since it was unanimously rejected by an advisory group of international experts in 1970. The plan indeed has its shortcomings, but because of the experts' violent criticism, its positive features have often been overlooked. In several respects, the Master Plan demonstrates the same shared awareness of Jerusalem's special qualities which was common to all the mandatory and Israeli plans of the past. The plan's basic physical premise, that the city should have a clearly defined edge, surrounded by a green belt of open space, is solidly within the tradition of previous plans. The manner in which this premise is developed in the Master Plan would give the city visual and functional coherence: Jerusalem would fill out the 'city space' of its mountain-top plateau, and the city's edge would therefore be clearly defined by the steep slopes surrounding the plateau. In the area of the Old City particularly, the Master Plan shows an awareness of and sympathy for the principles of the past. The open space proposed around the Old City is more generous than in most of the previous plans. In its general outline, the Master Plan's Old City open space resembles that of Holliday's 1934 plan, although its proposals are in fact more extensive than Holliday's. Significantly, the plan defines the area as a nature reserve rather than as a landscaped park, and in this respect also it resembles Holliday's concept. It should be recalled that the previous statutory plan for the Old City area, done by Kendall in 1964 for the Jordanian authorities, had zoned the entire area for residential use.

If in some ways the Master Plan's concepts made a positive contribution to the cumulative dialogue which has characterized the building of the city, in other ways it showed a spirit which the city had not seen since the Romans laid out Aelia Capitolina's grid-iron over the ruins of Herod's Jerusalem. The major weakness of the Master Plan lay in a choice of goals, many of which were not compatible with the existing form and character of the city nor with its social heritage. A simplistic physical and social unity were to be imposed upon a city whose essence had been the variety and separateness of its communities. A dense commercial core serving a large metropolitan region was to be implanted upon a city with an existing linear commercial centre and an antiquated radial-concentric system of narrow streets. The new road system providing access to the commercial core would have required the destruction of large portions of the existing city. The system also would have imposed large-scale roads and interchanges upon the Old City's landscape. The total physical image which the plan projected was not a sympathetic one: dense residential districts, much larger and more solidly-packed than in any previous plan, faced each other across narrow strips of open space, which were themselves merely the corridors of the new road system. The intention which lay behind the proposal of a unified city, focused upon a single commercial centre and bound together by a grid-iron of new roads, was a political one. Its goal was to physically express, and thereby help to bring about, a united Israeli Jerusalem. This unity was to be imposed contrary to the city's functional capacities and financial limitations, and at the expense of many aesthetic and environmental qualities.

Town planning used to achieve political and economic ends is certainly nothing new; it is a common and not always negative procedure. History is full of instances of the successful imposition of a new order upon an existing situation, but the new order has always drawn its basic features from the nature of the place. Versailles would never have been built in the Judean Mountains, nor would Baron Haussmann have cut his Boulevards through Jerusalem's domed hills and meandering valleys.

The Master plan, in some of its concepts, and other, much worse plans for Jerusalem demonstrate a new and alien tendency. The fundamental, commonly-shared awareness that Jerusalem's spiritual essence is inextricably bound up with her visual, tangible qualities, an awareness evidenced by four thousand years of building in the city, is now not simply ignored, it is not even recognized. Instead, a new way of thinking about Jerusalem has sprung up: the city is a resource to be exploited, its spiritual and visual qualities are commodities to be bought and sold. The authorities, in order to raise ready cash, have been selling away the city's visual and symbolic heritage. Architects, members of the third, the 'know-nothing' generation of modern architecture, finding this way of thinking not at all uncongenial, have eagerly joined in building for Jerusalem as if she were the moon.

Effects of contemporary planning ideology (88, 90) on the fabric of the city.

88 View to Central London from Parliament Hill.

89 Westminster Abbey.

90 Knightsbridge Barracks by Sir Basil Spence.

91 Kensington Gardens.

# III Two philosophies

*'Thy silver is become dross, thy wine mixed with water'*

THE PROCESS WHICH is now beginning to alter Jerusalem's basic form and character is similar to a process which has been occurring in many other cities throughout the world. It is a new kind of urban growth and represents a new way of thinking about the nature and function of cities, and of the buildings within them. The ideology by which modern architecture and modern town-planning justify their participation in this process traces its origins to the earliest works and writings of the modern movement in the last decades of the nineteenth century. It was further elaborated after the first World War, setting in motion creative energies which reached their fruition in the 1930s. By mid-century the forms and concepts that had evolved came to be whole-heartedly endorsed by government and corporate entities throughout the Western World, and took on the status of an official style, manifesting the intuitive agreement between architect and patron which had characterized the great architectural styles of the past. In isolated instances great architecture was produced, but for the most part the official style resulted in gigantic, ill-functioning, and desolate complexes which began to ravage the centres of European cities in the late 1960s, repeating a process which had occurred in American cities during the previous decade. This late form of the style and its ideology still bore some resemblance to the pioneering work of half a century before, but it ignored and negated at least one of the original and basic premises of modern architecture.

Frank Lloyd Wright's work and his writings had emphasized an organic relation between building and site. For Wright, the qualities of

90

91

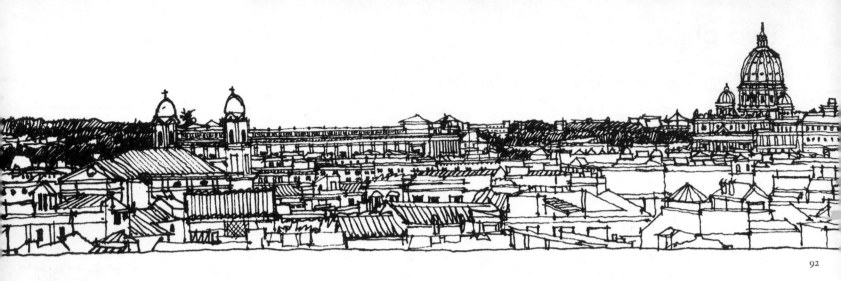

92

93

the site were basic determinants of architectural form. The landscape was treated not merely as the backdrop for a building; the two were made to interpenetrate to form a new organic unity. Mies van der Rohe's conception of architecture recognized the primacy of the site in a different way. Mies had reduced architecture to the simplest and clearest expression of its fundamental elements: his buildings were 'skin and bones'. With the lightness and elegance of their structure and their maximum transparency, they became in effect the settings for their surroundings. Mies's genius in relating building to site is perhaps best shown in the design of the Seagram's Building and its piazza on Park Avenue in New York City.

But the creation of an organic, or lyrical, or civilized relation between buildings and their surroundings is no longer an important goal of the ideology of the official style. In fact, the ideology in its current form makes it extremely difficult for its proponents to even recognize the essential visual and emotional qualities of a place, be it a landscape or an existing city fabric, let alone to design sympathetically within it.

It is this narrowness of vision, rather than a conscious wish to destroy, which explains much of what is now happening in Jerusalem

92  The skyline of Rome from the Villa Medici.

93  The Martin House, Buffalo, New York by Frank Lloyd Wright, 1904.

58

94

and elsewhere. The ideology which produces this blindness is a powerful and seductive one; it has influenced a whole generation of modern architects, men who are supposed to be professionally involved with visual matters, but who, in Le Corbusier's words, possess 'eyes which do not see'.

By the mid-1960s another approach was being articulated by younger architects. In doing so, they were continuing the thread which ran through the work of the lonely few of the older generation who were in fact the profession's finest practitioners. Included below are brief statements of attitude from each viewpoint about ways of thought and perception; about history, aesthetics, values, nature and the design process, followed by a resumé of each ideology's view of Jerusalem. Both arguments are stated in the extreme form in which they are often encountered. Neither is wholly consistent, and both may contain logical as well as factual errors. The purpose of contrasting these viewpoints is a practical, not an epistemologic one. It is to show how an ideology produces a way of seeing, thinking, and building, and how, if this way of building is to change to meet our real needs, the ideology which underlies it must be replaced with a different kind of awareness.

## Ways of thought and perception
### The Deductive Approach

*The ideology of the official style sees reality in terms of basic abstractions which are developed into usable concepts through a process of deductive reasoning. It characteristically searches for the pure essences behind the immediate world of sense data, and arrives at these abstractions by a process of isolation, concentration, and reduction. The isolation of an object of thought or of perception involves conceptually removing it from its specific and accidental spatial and temporal context. Key aspects which relate directly to the purposes of the investigation are concentrated upon, and by the process of reduction all superficial and irrelevant detail, i.e. all the specific and unique qualities of an object including its emotive and symbolic associations, are thought away, and its pure, true, and universal essence is arrived at.*

*This philosophy is, however, not concerned with the contemplation of Abstract Truth: it is a base for action. The existing situation must be made to conform to the ideal, and the ideal is an abstraction, it is verbal, or numerical, and without sense content. Man overpowers a hostile world and a recalcitrant past; he re-moulds it in the image of his abstract reason. The thought processes are one-way (as are the political processes) from the top down. 'Cogito ergo sum – L'état c'est moi.'*

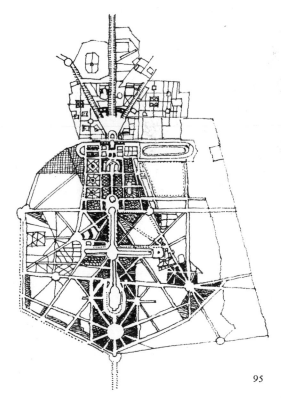

95

94 The London skyline: St Paul's Cathedral and the results of the Greater London Council's 'high building' policy.

95 Plan of Versailles.

59

96  View of Paris, 1973.

*Specific entities deduced from abstractions – for example, a building project – are considered in isolation from their existent surroundings, since these surroundings are irrational and inefficient. The existent is considered, in effect, 'tabula rasa'. Acts and events are discrete, cause and effect are a linear, one way process. Reality is simple and one-dimensional. The intrusion of another dimension of reality into this process is prevented at the outset by defining all other possible dimensions as essentially unreal.*

## The Inductive and Empirical Approach

A workable idea of reality and one which results in workable and liveable cities and in an architecture which is to be loved as well as used is an idea which grants to immediate sense data, in all its irreducible concreteness, at least the same status of reality as is normally given to abstract concepts. The everyday perceptions of an individual, his direct experiences of his surroundings, have a validity which may in some cases out-balance the rates of economic growth projected ten years hence. Specific entities, buildings or town plans, should be considered as organic parts of interrelated perceptual wholes, and must be dealt with in terms of all of their perceivable and thinkable relations. These relations involve, among other things, people's feelings and sentiments about historical and symbolic values, as well as the effects of noise, dust, carbon monoxide, and sulphur dioxide upon the human organism. They also include the basic human desire for harmony, coherence, and the sense of identification with a place.

Acts and events, planned and unplanned, are threads in a fabric, parts of a spatial and temporal continuum, with multi-levels of meaning and importance. This interwoven texture may, in some of its aspects, be simulated mathematically, and computers may be used to analyse it and predict some of its directions. For other equally important aspects, multi-levels of perception should be encouraged. This involves the transference of thought and awareness from an exclusive concern with isolated objects and situations, to a thinking about and perceiving of concrete organic wholes. This kind of perception is made all the more difficult by the cacophony of urban life, and by the manipulative pressures of the mass media which attempt to direct consciousness toward isolated particulars which we are supposed to purchase and consume. But the perception of inter-related wholes is not a special skill, or an occult exercise: the evidence provided by nearly all of man's visual history (until recently) shows that it is a natural mode of human awareness.

## Attitude toward History
### The Deductive Approach

*The iron law of History dictates that architecture reflect the philosophy of its age, its technology, and the state of its arts. Ours is an age of materialism, of unprecedented economic growth, and of scientific and technical wonders. Our visual arts are abstract and highly idiosyncratic, having long since broken with the past. Our architecture must not only continue to reflect these characteristics, it should continue the attempt to give unified expression to the diverse tendencies of the Spirit of the Times. Just as Baroque architecture embodied the Baroque spirit, its mathematics, its music, its painting and sculpture, so modern architecture can perform the great service of bridging the gap between science and art by giving physical, artistic expression to the rationalist tendencies of our age, and thus become its unifying symbol. Large, high-density, high-rise complexes, traffic architecture and 'megastructure' schemes are all evidence of a new age being born, of a new way of life and of new priorities and values. It is our duty to the Zeitgeist to help bring these courageous new projects about. Even if they do not appeal to us personally, we have no right to question their validity and necessity. The general public, with its lack of historical perspective, and its sentimental, reactionary and philistine taste, does not appreciate the grandeur of this vision. But the public was always short-sighted. The Eiffel Tower was condemned in its time, as was probably the Parthenon. Great art which is ahead of its time has always been attacked by the insensitive and the narrow-minded. Finally, it should be emphasized that the present renewal of our cities has numerous parallels in the past. Baroque Rome, for example, was largely built of marble stripped from the ancient monuments of Imperial Rome, yet no one now accuses the Baroque architects of being barbarians.*

## The Inductive Approach

The Zeitgeist will take care of itself. Whatever we build will express our age. We are certainly under no obligation to impose alien and unworkable forms upon our cities in order to facilitate future historians' analysis of the forces underlying our times. The concept of historical determinism by which the deductive approach justifies its architecture was inherited from a group of nineteenth century Teutonic dialecticians, and is itself timebound and of limited application. If it is possible to discern a fundamental tendency of our age, it is perhaps not the working-out of History's iron laws, but the freedom of choice and action which the technological inventiveness and economic resources of our time give us. The supposed inevitability of modern architecture's forms, and of the economic and technical forces behind them, often effectively silences criticism, but it is perhaps the most questionable feature in the deductive ideology. The attitudes, policies and decisions which have produced this architecture are not natural laws, nor do they represent historical inevitability. They belong to the man-made world of choice, and they can be changed. The contemporary awareness of history differs from those of the past. The Renaissance and the nineteenth century in particular took certain historic periods as sources of inspiration, while ignoring or sometimes depreciating others. History for us represents an interrelated continuum. The cumulative built record of this continuum, which is expressed in the contemporary city's fabric of ordinary buildings as well as in its monuments, deserves to be treated with some measure of respect. The great surgical operations now being performed upon this fabric are unprecedented in their scale and character. They are not, as in

Baroque Rome, despoiling the deserted ruins of ancient monuments in the service of a new aesthetic vision. These operations are tearing out the hearts of living, functioning cities and replacing them with randomly related complexes whose purpose is in any event not the realization of a new aesthetic vision, but rather of maximum return on investment.

Modern architecture is stylistically and ideologically at the same point in its evolution as was nineteenth century Eclecticism at the end of its course; it deals in misplaced analogies and empty abstractions, and has become blind to the needs and realities of its time. Just as most architects in the late nineteenth century ignored the realities of the emerging forces of engineering technology and devoted their attention to clothing their buildings in archaeologically correct 'styles', so modern architects, concerned with the sculptural qualities of individual buildings standing in abstract space, ignore the pressing social, environmental and ecologic issues involved in their projects. From a technological point of view, modern architecture's current large-scale efforts are hardly avant-garde, or particularly courageous. The structural concepts involved are thirty or even fifty years old, and their technical execution represents a kind of mindless grinding-out of thoroughly familiar elements. The dismal and dispirited quality which these projects often convey probably reflects the lack of excitement involved in their design.

## Aesthetics
### The Deductive Approach

*The aesthetic features of modern architecture have two functions to fulfil. The first has already been alluded to; it is to express in architectural form the essential nature or spirit of the times. This is done first of all simply to help make people aware that they are living in a period vastly different from all previous ones. An awareness and acceptance of this fact will help promote further progress. But the aesthetic values of modern architecture have a more important function to fulfil. By giving architectural expression to certain abstract notions, these* aesthetic devices allow people to appreciate in a subjective and immediate way the great objective facts and tendencies of our age. For example, relativity physics or quantum mechanics are understood by a very few of us, yet they are central features of our scientific thinking. Modern architecture, by devising new ways of treating space and structure, has been able to produce tangible metaphors for these scientific concepts. The same kind of process applies to the relation between architecture and the other visual arts. The visual arts of our time have been generally characterized by a search for essences, and for new ways of perceiving and of feeling, unencumbered by reference to the limits of ordinary sense perception. Modern architecture attempts to express this attitude in its handling of structure, space, and materials, and thus is bringing about that unity of thought and feeling, of art and science which has characterized the great ages of the past.

The second function fulfilled by the aesthetic features of modern architecture is to allow a new range of freedom of artistic expression to the individual architect. Modern architecture has dispensed with the academic rules of the past, and allows each designer the opportunity of developing his own personal style, to an unprecedented degree. This may seem to contradict the logical and universal tendencies of modern architecture, but the individualistic expressions of the style are wholly consistent with a basic theme of our age: the realization of individual freedom. One may disagree with the specific designs produced, but the principle of self-expression in architecture is sacred. It often results in an interesting variety in our city scape.

Both the objective and the personal varieties of aesthetic expression make use of abstract space and abstract structure. Nineteenth century revivalism employed symbolic and associative devices to produce aesthetic effects not normally encountered in architecture. These literary and historical devices were swept away by the modern pioneers, who began to use space and structure as artistic elements in their own right. The progress made in modern painting gives an insight into how space and structure are now used in architecture. Firstly, abstract painting dispensed with the representation of objects, and presented instead colours and shapes as the subject matter. A further step forward was taken when the actual paint itself, its texture and treatment, became the subject of the painting. In a similar way, space and structure themselves are the 'subjects' of architectural expression. Great architecture of the past has also used space and structure in an abstract manner, particularly that of ancient Greece, and of the Renaissance.

One of the finest characteristics of modern architecture is the way in which its buildings relate to their surroundings. If a large modern building is placed next to older, smaller structures, the very contrast often heightens the beauty and delicacy of the old buildings. But more important, the juxtaposition of scales, and of old and new, creates among people a new level of awareness about their surroundings. If two objects not normally encountered together, objects from very different worlds, are juxtaposed, a kind of creative shock value is produced. The tension brought about by this juxtaposition produces a new kind of reality in which both objects have been transformed in our consciousness and have taken on new meanings. In this way, our awareness of our environment has risen to a higher plane.

We cannot often count upon creative interaction between old and new. We should, however, also be grateful for the occasional works of genius which simply rise above the humdrum level of prosaic architecture. It is these occasional works of artistic merit which compensate for the great mass of faceless and monotonous buildings which make up our cities.

The Inductive Approach

Architecture is a tangible art which defines and creates specific places which are to be lived in or used. Its aesthetic impact comes from its direct physical presence, from a sense of containment, of balance and counterbalance, of movement, of light and shadow, of mass, of surface and texture, and of scale. Its sense impact involves not only visual relations but also sound and touch. The total experience is also bound-up with certain meanings. But these meanings are not, strictly speaking, 'symbolized' or 'represented' by the experience,

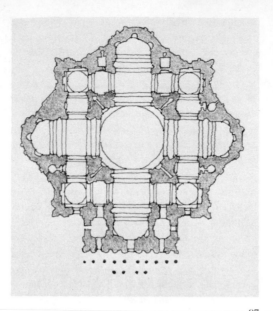

97

they are embodied within it. Because of our verbally oriented culture, this is for many people a difficult point to grasp. Traditionally, works of architecture were seldom, if ever, considered as syllogisms to be understood or as puzzles to be solved, but as structural and spatial organisms to be experienced in an immediate physical way. Greek architecture evolved over centuries a series of mathematical relationships and physical forms (the orders) whose purpose was to evoke a visual sense of harmony and equilibrium. The temples were richly carved and brightly-coloured: they were to be sensed as bodily presences, not understood as concepts. Renaissance architecture's undoubted neo-platonic associations did not result in abstractness. The concepts which formed the architecture were themselves tied to sense experience, they were geometric 'concrete universals'; the circle, the cross axis, the central plan.

In the nineteenth century, architecture began to be used to express concepts or attitudes in a wholly abstract, or in a literal and representational way. Buildings were to be understood rather than sensed. The concepts expressed still had their base in the world of experience – the power and majesty of the state, a nostalgia for the past, etc. In contemporary architecture, an attempt has been made to communicate concepts for which there is no physical correlative (relativity physics) or no objective reference (the private notions of the architect). Beyond this, space or structure in itself are being expressed, purified of all romantic, superficial, and associative encumbrances.

The attempt to embody architecturally the concepts of contemporary physics has generally been futile. There is no conflict between architecture and quantum mechanics, they simply deal with very different things in very different ways. The personal notions of the architect may find a universal expression if the architect is highly gifted, but for the most part, the personal notions remain private.

In its practical effects, the architectural attempt to express scientific concepts simply confuses scientific and mathematical space with perceptual space. The particularly bleak and

97 Michelangelo's plan for St Peter's in Rome. '*Great architecture of the past used space and structure abstractly*', say the deductivists. But, on the inductive view, the concepts which formed this architecture were 'concrete universals': the circle, the cross axis and the central plan.

desolate aspect which it usually takes on reflects the emptiness of the abstractions with which it deals. On the other hand, that half of the modern ideology which stresses self-expression at the expense of a common language of architecture often produces a visual incoherence which can be even more monotonous than the faceless and placeless results of the more objective ideology. The individualistic efforts are usually not only irresponsible from an urban design standpoint, they also express a specious and superficial individuality. The programmatic and economic decisions which give a building its essential form are not made by architects, but by their corporate clients. Thus, both kinds of mono-tony stem from the same essential fact: the architect has ceased to determine, except in the most superficial aspects, the form of buildings, and has become a mere technician in the service of his corporate and governmental masters. Ironically enough, this has come about because corporate and governmental clients have become wholly convinced of what was once a revolutionary doctrine of the modern movement – that architecture must be a wholly rational, technical exercise.

The last kind of expression, that of space itself, stripped of irrelevancies, has often resulted in scaleless and non-human volumes. It was the 'superfluous' elements, organically bound within the total spatial concept, which produced the great spaces of past architecture.

The way in which the products of the deductive approach relate, or fail to relate to their built and natural surroundings points out the approach's greatest lack: its inability to

98

99

98 'Temple of Neptune' at Paestum, fifth century B C. 'Architecture is a bodily presence to be sensed, not a puzzle to be solved.'

99 The Yale Arts and Architecture Building, by Paul Rudolph, 1963.
*'We should be grateful for the occasional works of genius which simply rise above the humdrum level of prosaic architecture.'*

grasp the basic notion of a city as an organically interconnected fabric. The Surrealist arguments endorsing the value of shock in expanding consciousness are, like modern architecture's technical concepts, decades old, and have not improved with time. Even if the Surreal vision were realized, it would be an irresponsible exercise in manipulation. The use of this device may be appropriate for painting, collage or film, where one has a choice of viewing or not viewing a work. It is however out of place in town-planning. It reflects a totalitarian, or at best excessively paternalistic attitude. The ordinary citizen should be allowed to select his own shocks.

Modern architecture has unquestionably produced works of genius. What it has failed to produce is a common approach to building which, in less skilled hands, will result in solutions which are appropriate to their context. At present, the creation of isolated works of brilliance is perhaps less crucial than building, in our own way, a civilized and humanly-scaled continuation of our existing environment.

**Attitude toward values**

The Deductive Approach

*A study of history shows that notions of value arise out of the inevitable forces of the age. Strictly speaking, we cannot objectively question these forces since they have made us what we are. We should, however, guide our actions by realistically appraising these forces and adjusting ourselves to them. This adjustment is necessary since we all retain a residue of outmoded values from a previous age. Historical forces represent neither an absolute Good nor an Evil, since absolute values are non-existent. They represent rather a morally neutral phenomenon which can be used to our advantage if properly understood. The social sciences tell us that our personal values are relative to our cultural and social environment. Clearly, our personal reactions are no basis for judging these great historical tendencies. The model we should follow*

100 The Albert Memorial, London, 1863.
'In the nineteenth century, architecture began to be used to express concepts and attitudes in an abstract or in a literal and representational way.'

101 Glyptothek, Munich, 1815–34.

is the value-free analytical method of science. To achieve scientific objectivity, we should as far as possible try to deal with quantifiable data in order to eliminate our subjective bias. Our approach to problems should thus be technical and objective, rather than moral and personal.

This should not be taken to mean that modern architects and town-planners have no values. The technical approach implies certain ethical norms. The ability to look at reality squarely, without bias, and to act accordingly requires honesty and perseverance. The way in which modern architects design reflects this honesty. The analogy of the growth of a flower may be used to show how concepts are evolved from an honest and objective appraisal of reality. The flower grows and ultimately unfolds according to the working-out of its own inner necessity, contained implicitly within the seed. The principle of its form determines all its parts and their relation to one another, and this principle is in itself an expression of how the flower 'works', how it functions and grows. The best of modern architecture follows in its design a similar process, unfolding its structure and its spaces according to the inner logic of its functions. The result is an inevitable and necessary beauty, like that of the flower, or conversely, like the solid and virtuous beauty of the finest works of engineering. The attempt to apply irrelevant external restraint to the integral unfolding of an architectural concept is invalid. This was shown long ago when the false and superfluous 'façadism' of the nineteenth century was replaced by modern architecture's honesty. The very ugliness of most late nineteenth-century architecture was proof of its dishonesty.

Another ethical norm central to the practice of modern architecture is a sense of duty to the client. The architect as a professional is obligated to respect his client's will and to realize his intentions. Clearly, the architect must retain his value-free attitude and not allow his private notions to interfere with his professional dealings. Similarly, the architect has a responsibility to his colleagues in the profession and must refrain from any public criticism of them.

Finally, it must be pointed out that works of architecture cannot be judged on the basis of the supposed morality or immorality of their purposes. The Colosseum and the Baths of Caracalla in Rome

102

102 Nash's Carlton House Terrace, 1827. 'Architecture as part of the organic fabric of the city'.

## The Inductive Approach

The modernist ideology in its discussion of values characteristically deduces categorical statements from abstract concepts, and forgets its own concrete traditions. In keeping with the inductive approach, we should look at these traditions, and then see where they have led in order to understand the implications of what the modernists are trying to say about values in architecture.

'The school of architecture has two aims: to train the architect by imparting the necessary knowledge and skills, and to educate him in order that he can make proper use of the knowledge and skills he has acquired. Thus training has practical purposes in view, but education has values. It is the business of education to implant insight and responsibility . . . Any introduction to the problems of city planning must teach the fundamentals on which it is based, and show clearly how all aspects of building are interconnected and related to the city as an organism.'

Mies van der Rohe

The modern movement began as a fervent rebellion against the hypocrisy and thinly veiled brutality of the culture which ultimately produced the horrors of the First World War. After the war, the movement took on new force and became even more deeply involved in social as well as aesthetic issues. Countless schemes, both visionary and practical, proposed a fundamental reorganization of the physical environment in order to realize humanitarian goals. However, by the time modern architecture had become the official

103  The flower: a deductive view.

104  The flower: an empirical, inductive view.

style, its moral component had been reduced to a servile obedience to its new clients. These clients represented something unprecedented in the history of economic organization. The personal despotism of the robber barons had been replaced by the expertise of the *apparatchiks* and of the professional managers. Correspondingly, the modern movement's social messianism has given way to the 'value-free' exercise of power and of technique.

It should be clear that modern architecture as currently practised does indeed manifest a set of values. The conflict now taking place in our cities shows the nature of these values. The conflict itself is not between an objective tendency on the one hand and moral and sentimental notions on the other. It is between two conflicting kinds of interests; the one general and public, the other private and particularistic. The sense of outrage at the destruction of the organic visual order of our cities, and at the resultant congestion and general inconvenience is at least as real and objective as the moral neutrality of the developers' profit chart and of the architect's fee calculation.

The analogy of the flower illustrates the narrowness and particularity of the deductive approach. The flower is taken out of its context, it is torn out of the earth and examined under the surgical lamp of abstract reasoning in an attempt to discover the secret of its unfolding. The flower's form is seen as the result of an inner mechanism. The basic fact about the flower is forgotten: that it grows in a specific place, and that its structure and the pattern of its growth are an expression of an evolutionary process of inner adjustment to the realities of its surroundings. The flower's interaction with the specific qualities of soil and climate produce its form, and give it life.

The deductive ideology's narrow approach is also found in the modernist's conception of the architect's professional role. The physician's duty to his patient does not involve allowing the patient to dictate his own treatment. The architect is obligated to guide the client according to his professional knowledge, and one of the main components in this guidance

must be a consideration of the larger consequences of a proposal. If the term 'profession' is to have any meaning in relation to the practice of architecture, it must encompass a sense of responsibility to society as well as to the client. Most architects and certainly all town-planners should, on the basis of their professional experience, be able to assess the environmental impact of a scheme upon its context, and this assessment should influence their decision of how to build, or indeed, whether to build at all.

Moral judgments about architecture are often highly questionable, and should be made with great care. It is reasonable to maintain that present moral opinion about a building's past uses can be irrelevant to its architectural merit. As regards monuments of the past whose purposes we may condemn (the Colosseum, the Mayan Sacrificial Pyramids, etc.), it should however be pointed out that these purposes were considered at the time as representing the highest values of society, and thus worthy of monumental expression. The brilliance and grandeur of their designs reflected this attitude. Few people would maintain that property speculation deserves to be expressed as the noblest activity of our time. Nor do the technical and artistic qualities of the speculative monuments compare with those of the past. It is not the morality of property speculation that is presently being questioned, but rather the inappropriate expression it receives, and the detrimental effect that this expression has on other, more important values.

What are the more important values? There are, of course, a whole series of technical and economic arguments against the unrestrained application of 'value-free' planning, but these arguments are, it must be said, irrelevant to a discussion of values. Values are the standards by which other things are measured. In their ultimate form they cannot be further explained by other qualities or purposes. Logically speaking, they are absolutes. From an empirical point of view, on the basis of common human experience, it seems permissible to say that nature, and the man-made landscape in its

105 The flower and the Temple Mount, where it
grows.

finest form, as well as the historically-cumulative works of man all have an intrinsic value, a spritual worth which goes beyond questions of their monetary and functional value, and of their potential uses. In human terms, these are 'Public Goods', they affect us all and they 'belong' to us all, they are our common heritage. Their 'function' is to elevate the human spirit.

## Jerusalem
The Deductive Approach

*Essentially, Jerusalem is a place where each period of history has expressed its values and its way of building. We have not only the right, but also the obligation to add our own characteristic contribution to the city's history by applying those principles of architecture and town-planning which are universally valid for our age. The universality of architectural forms and concepts is an essential feature of the philosophy of modern design. Solutions which have grown 'out of the nature of the problem' and which have evolved according to the inner necessities of functional and technological demands, can and should be applied universally. This is so because the true nature of our time lies not in the accidents of specific place and circumstance, but in the development of universally valid technological processes and economic forms of organization. The replacement of the irrational and the specific by the general and the logical has the important result of breaking down national and racial barriers and promoting common understanding by creating a common environment.*

*In order to properly assess and adequately provide for the city's future needs, town-planning in Jerusalem must follow the objective procedures of contemporary planning methodology.*

*Briefly, this methodology eliminates the planner's subjective bias by basing programmes for the city's future development upon projections of statistical data concerning present rates of population growth, economic expansion, rates of motorization, etc. These objectively quantified programmes may also allow for certain non-quantifiable historical and sentimental elements which in certain instances may*

*influence details of the programme. On the basis of this programme, a series of test solutions are developed, and the one which optimizes the programme's requirements is chosen for implementation.*

*It is of course impossible to predict in advance the precise form that Jerusalem will take as a result of this process, since it is not intended to produce any preconceived form, but to allow the fulfilment of essential needs. The form of the city will be the inevitable result of its economic and technical processes. Thus contemporary town-planning does not try to emulate the city-forms of the past, with their static, set-piece urban designs. It produces instead a new kind of open-ended and dynamic city form whose essence is to be found primarily in its inner process, and only secondarily in its external appearance. The philosophical depth of this concept makes it a worthy successor to the spiritual qualities of Jerusalem's development.*

*In practical terms, Jerusalem will become an expanding, progressive commercial centre, a modern city, worthy to be the capital of Israel. Jerusalem's present form, quaint and pastoral though it may be, is not adequate to its new importance. Of course, the Old City itself, in its physical make-up, should be preserved, but its functions and its character should be up-graded in accordance with its commercial and touristic potential. This is not to say that Jerusalem will not be a beautiful place. The contrast of old and new will heighten the beauty of both. Equally important, contemporary planning methods, and building technology will give Jerusalem's citizens new employment opportunities, modern housing, convenient commercial facilities, and freedom of movement.*

The Inductive Approach

The way in which we build the Jerusalem of our era should manifest the finest and most constructive tendencies of our age, and not its destructive forces. The application of deductivist planning concepts and the imposition of its building forms upon Jerusalem's fabric will not result in simply another addition to the city's long history of building. The sheer quantities involved, the vast scale and bulk of the projects proposed would result in an unprecedented change in the city's form. Our age seems prepared to carry out what no other era would have permitted; in order to achieve purposes alien to the city's heritage, we shall, at a single stroke, cancel out a tradition of building thousands of years old.

The demand that Jerusalem become a 'modern city' ignores the basic fact that the modern city 'shows unmistakable signs of disintegration through physical waste, pollution, and environmental erosion, as well as through rising incidence of disease, drug addiction, crime and psychotic violence'. (From Lewis Mumford's letter to the Jerusalem Committee, November 1970.) Experience in other cities has thus shown that the modernist vision of high density and unrestrained technology does not result in an expression of the highest ideals of our age. What these ideals may be has been previously indicated. They include a unique awareness of and respect for the built records of man's cumulative history, as well as the recognition of individual and collective freedom of choice. Our technology and our economic resources give us the freedom to show restraint, and this restraint will be our contribution to Jerusalem's history.

Jerusalem's organic vernacular of building provides a fine example of a fundamental characteristic of the art of architecture – the way in which the specific quality of a place, its light, its materials, topography, climate, vegetation and history (including technological history) are instinctively understood and reflected in the spatial organization, the structural order, and in the use of materials, textures, and colours. Architecture can bring together specific givens in a non-transferable way to produce a universal expression. The indiscriminate application of universal form and technology blots out this essential relation to the specific site and produces the well-known 'placelessness' of the modernist vision. This vision is clearly inadmissible in Jerusalem.

It is essential that in Jerusalem the standard methodology by which quantified programmes and plans are produced be replaced by another approach. The deductive method dismisses as subjective or virtually ignores all planning determinants which involve human perceptions or feelings, and which therefore cannot be readily quantified. In doing so, it fails to recognize fully needs and requirements whose fulfilment should be one of planning's basic goals. Deductive planning may pay lip service to its regard for 'sentimental' and aesthetic needs, but these are seldom formulated as part of the programme in a way which allows them to hold their own against quantified purposes. Whenever there is a conflict between quantified 'objective' requirements and qualitative 'subjective' ones, the methodology, if left to itself, will invariably sacrifice the latter to the former.

In Jerusalem, perhaps more than in any other city, qualitative and non-measurable forces have formed, and must continue to form the pattern of its urban growth. To continue this tradition, the methods of contemporary town-planning must be revised, and its priorities re-arranged. One method proposed has been to devise a way of quantifying the qualitative elements of urban life and urban form. Weighted according to their position in the total hierarchy of urban values, these qualities could effectively counter-balance the purely quantitative elements in determining planning priorities.

This is not a simple task. A satisfactory procedure has as yet not been devised, but work on it is proceeding which may in time completely alter the present methods of planning.

Another, more conventional method can be employed to help prevent the worst excesses of deductive planning and to promote a livable environment. This method involves the assessment of the capacity of a certain place for accommodating growth. Based on this capacity, acceptable rates of population growth and economic expansion can be arrived at, thus reversing the current procedure. There are essentially two kinds of limits which must be established. The first determines allowable densities of development according to physically and socially determined human needs. The number of people and amount of activity which a given piece of ground can support is a function of human tolerances and requirements

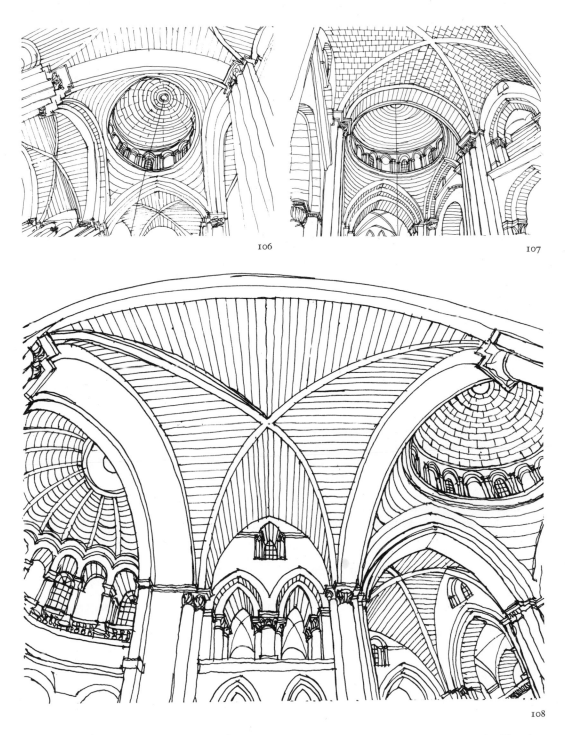

106

107

108

106, 107, 108 Interior views of the Holy Sepulchre. Architecture takes into account the history and the technological context of the specific place. The twelfth-century Crusader additions to the Church combine Gothic and Byzantine structural and stylistic elements.

(fresh air, light, privacy, quiet, social inter-action, etc.), and not of speculative land values. These tolerances and needs are not to be defined in terms of the limit of endurance, but as optimum values. Given adequate research, the whole procedure can, and in many cases has been quantified. In fact, this approach was once part of the classic modern ideology; it was then forgotten, and is now being slowly recalled.

The second kind of capacity to be established is derived from the specific qualities of the site. These include on the one hand its physical appropriateness for building, and the kind of functions it can best accommodate, based upon its position, topography, vegetation, soils and climate. This is an elementary procedure, and was also a central principle of modernist thought, but it too has recently been ignored. The other aspect of the specific capacity of a site involves its visual character, both in itself, and in relation to the larger perceptual structure of the city.

Because of the crucial role which specific visual determinates have played in Jerusalem's building tradition, it is clear that the definition of visual capacities in a way sympathetic to that tradition must continue to be a central feature in determining the city's future form. The reasons for this are not only visual. These capacities generally correspond to densities and building forms associated with a way of life which Jerusalemites consider appropriate and desirable.

A deductive Jerusalem would replace visual determinants with the inevitable operation of economic and technological necessity, leaving the city's form to chance. The deductivists are convinced that the logical integrity of their methodology will necessarily produce a new kind of beauty – the beauty of open-ended form and on-going process. In its abstractness, this contention is wholly consistent with the rest of the deductive ideology. Unfortunately if past experience is any guide, 'open-ended form' and 'on-going process' in concrete terms mean visual chaos and environmental desolation, as well as semi-lethal levels of pollution.

## The Method of Visual Analysis

Armchair aesthetics are out of place in Jeru-salem. For this reason, an inductive method based on the analysis of visual data was devel-oped as part of the study for the plan for the Central Business District (see below, p. 102). The method follows the general lines of the 'townscape' techniques, and of the work of Kevin Lynch. Its original purpose was to discover that elusive quality 'the spirit of the place', which architects of previous eras, work-ing within an organic tradition, and usually bound to a single unified cultural environment, had been able to recognize instinctively. Basically, this and similar techniques attempt to provide the modern architect with a new way of seeing, which is, of course, merely the old way of seeing in a more or less systematic form. Its desired result is to help lead architects out of the blindness into which their deductive ideology has forced them.

This is a particularly pressing need in Jeru-salem, not only because of the present threat to the city's form, but because her essential visual structure and unique spatial qualities are in some ways hard to grasp in terms of Western architectural concepts. Assuming one already knows how to look, one is still compelled to learn what to look for in order to appreciate the city's essential qualities. British Mandatory planners, and early Israeli architects, still familiar with traditional ways of architectural perception, were able to discover her secrets fairly quickly. Since then, a sharp break in this

109 A Western spatial enclosure; section through the Piazza San Marco in Venice; B Middle-eastern platform space; section through the Temple Mount and the Old City at the same scale as A; C Plan of the Piazza San Marco; D Plan of the Temple area.

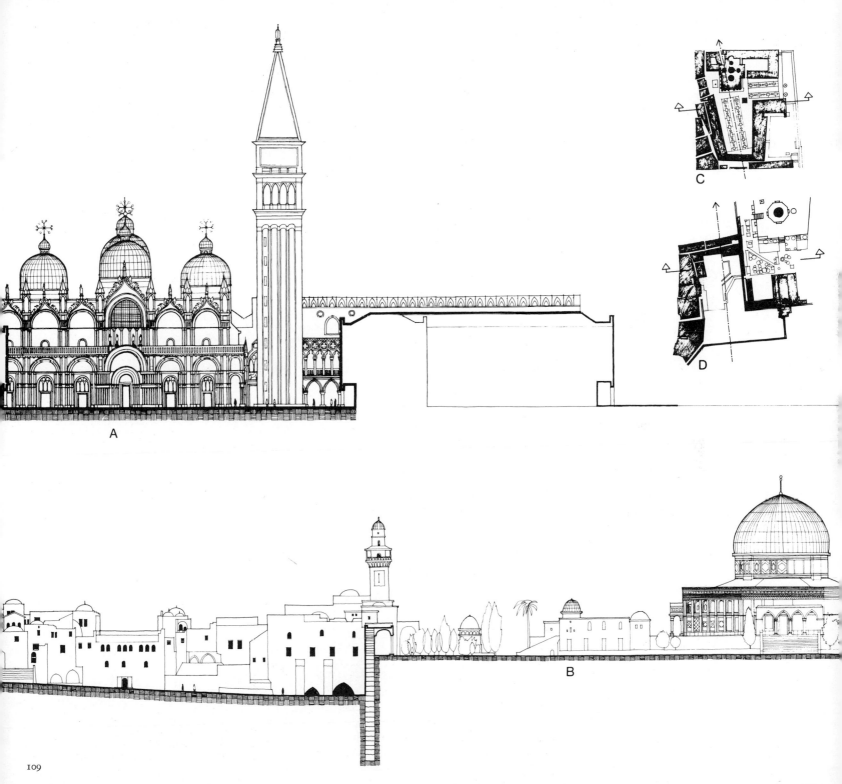

A

B

C

D

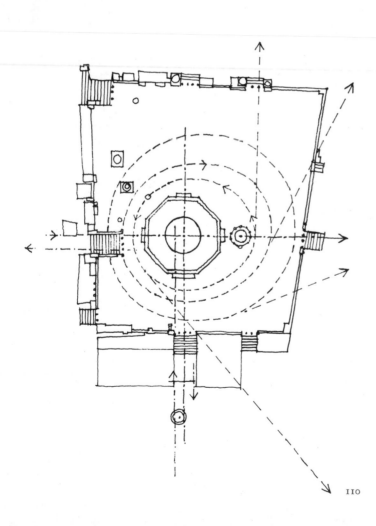

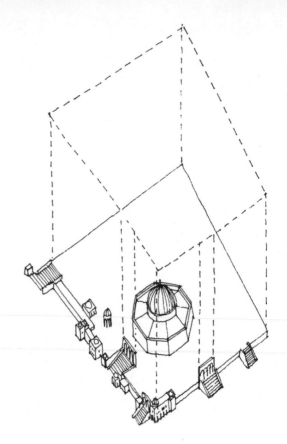

111

110

112

tradition has taken place, roughly corresponding with the rise of the official style.

Edmund Bacon, in his excellent and perceptive book *Design of Cities*, analyses the spatial quality of the platform of the Dome of the Rock. In doing so he shows how even a sensitive Western observer can overlook the essential nature of the place in the search for a familiar aesthetic. Bacon sees the free-standing arches which mark the entrances to the platform as defining a great shaft of space, ascending vertically from the platform and enveloping the dome. One can probably imagine such a spatial effect if one really tries, but the immediate perceptual space encountered on the platform is the visual bowl surrounding the Old City defined by its ring of hills. The mosque is the centre of gravity of this space, and the design and placement of the elements which surround it, the arches, and subsidiary structures on the platform, set up circular forces of movement around the dome. The arched gateways frame the mosque in their portals as we ascend the stairs to the platform. The slight but noticeable shifts of axis between these portals and the cardinal points of the mosque, strongly marked by its entrances, help set up 'spinning forces' which draw us into a circular movement around the mosque. This movement allows us to see the mosque. juxtaposed against the old city skyline, the surrounding hills, and the platform's small subsidiary structures. The circuit gives us the full sense of the mosque's centrality. This effect, and the elements used to achieve it are unlike those of Western spatial enclosure.

Jerusalem requires that we develop new ways of seeing. The techniques of visual analysis deal with the features which characterize the city's visual structure: skyline, panoramas, ensembles, spaces, sequences, key points, dominance and subdominance, scale and texture. The analysis divided the perception of the city into two categories, the static panoramic views, and the perception gained by moving through the city. Panoramic photos were taken from viewpoints which best revealed the city's total form, and these were converted into drawings, and analysed

through 'skyline diagrams'. The skyline diagrams were brought together to produce a 'composite skyline diagram' of the city as seen from its major viewpoints. This diagram was further analysed to determine the kind of forms and grouping which characterize the composite skylines, and to discover the key elements in the city's large scale form. The close range perceptions were recorded in the form of the city's major interior spaces, the movement patterns leading to them, and the key views associated with these movements. In this way, the central part of Jerusalem was found to consist of a series of 'perceptual wholes' – spaces and interlocking movement sequences. The analyses of panoramic views and of close range perceptions were combined to produce the 'dominance-subdominance' map. This map indicated the buildings which either dominated or punctuated the skyline, and also formed key points seen from within the city's space and movement systems. The map also assessed the relative range and power of these dominant and subdominant points.

The study had three major uses. It provided first of all a fairly comprehensive perceptual record of the central portion of the city, giving quick reference to the visual qualities of a given site in its relation to the whole area. Secondly, the panoramic drawings and diagrams were used to test the effect of specific building projects upon the surrounding cityscape, and the skyline. Thirdly, the analysis of spaces, sequences, and key views aided in the development of an open space and pedestrian system for the central area. Similar work was later done for the Old City area. Its visual space was defined, and key viewpoints and movement sequences were recorded.

The testing of proposed building projects by placing them in their panoramic context was the most rewarding and useful part of the study. It allowed architects and planners, and later the public, to gain an impression of a project's impact upon the total cityscape. In this way, certain *a priori* notions about the city's future form could be dispensed with. Conclusions about acceptable building height, mass, and scale, were thus empirically arrived at.

110 The slightly offset axes of the approaches to the Dome of the Rock produce 'spinning forces' which encourage the viewer to move around the Dome, thus seeing it against its background of the city and the hills.

111 Edmund Bacon's analysis: a cube of space rising from the Dome's platform.

112 View of the southern entrance to the Dome of the Rock.

113 Map of central Jerusalem with the panoramic
viewpoints used in the visual analysis of the city.
A  The Jaffa Gate; B  Shech Jarach; C  Abu-Tor;
D  Mount Zion.

114 Panoramic view from the Jaffa Gate (A) looking
west.

114

113

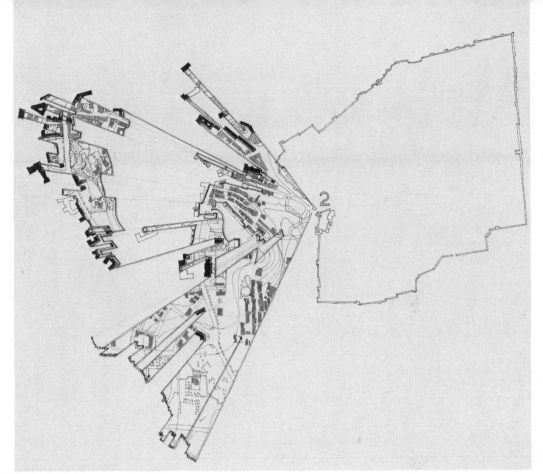

115 Diagram of the skyline and of the major groups of buildings and open spaces seen from the Jaffa Gate (2) in drawing 114.

115

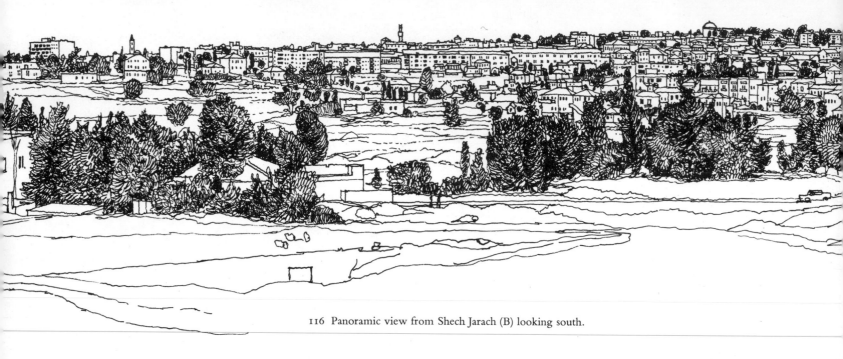

116 Panoramic view from Shech Jarach (B) looking south.

117 Panoramic view from Abu-Tor (C) looking north.

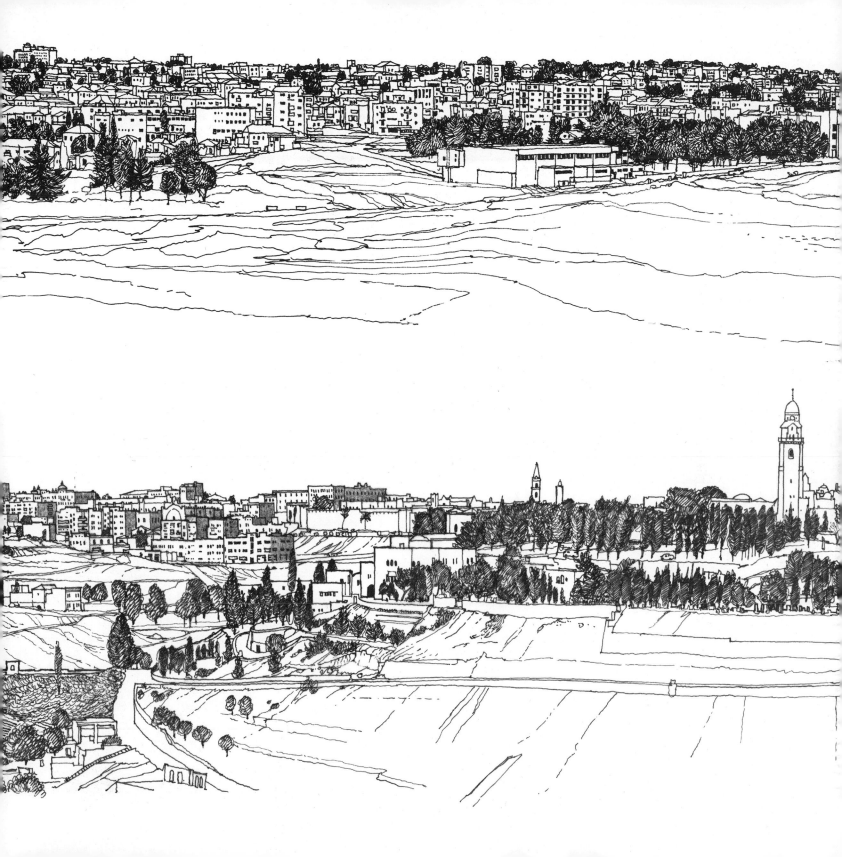

118 Panoramic view from Mount Zion (D) looking west.

119 The skyline diagrams of all the viewpoints around central Jerusalem were combined to produce a 'composite skyline diagram' of the area.

120 On the basis of the 'composite skyline diagram' a map has been produced showing the 'seen and unseen' areas of central Jerusalem. A The skyline ridges; B The unseen areas; C The major visible open spaces.

121 The 'perceptual wholes' of central Jerusalem. The hatching shows the visual limits of the city's major urban spaces.

122 The key viewpoints and movement sequences from which the urban spaces in diagram 121 are perceived.

119

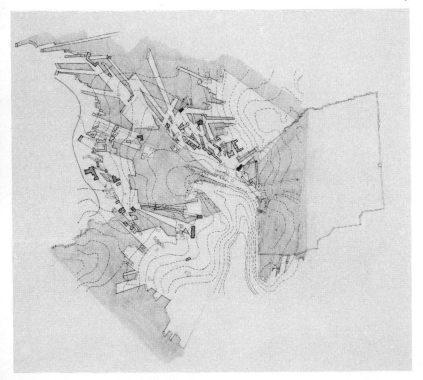

120

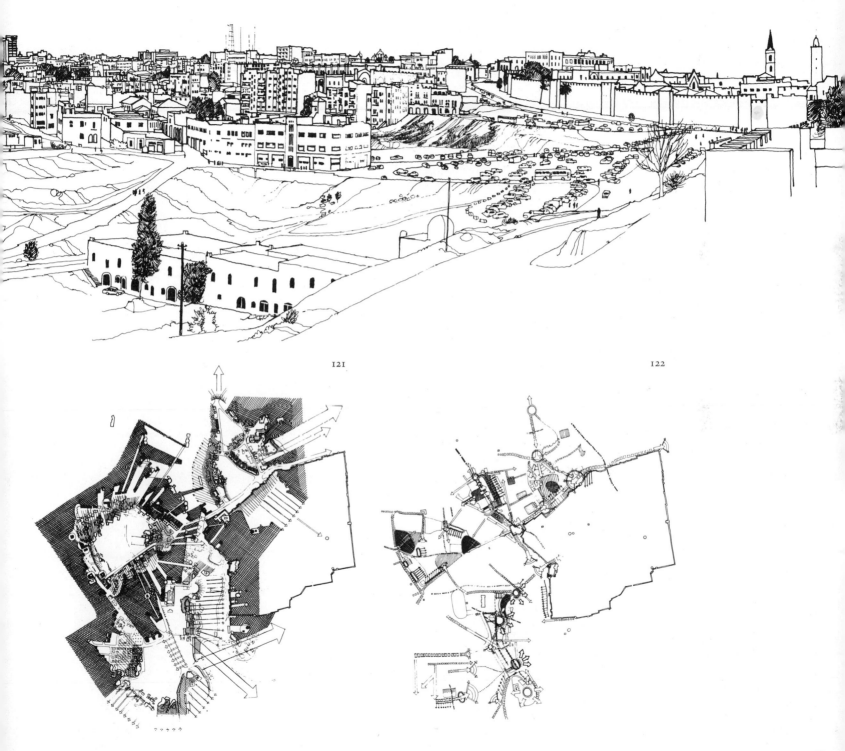

121

122

## Empirical Jerusalem

The techniques of visual analysis have helped to bring about the formulation of certain basic notions about the city's form and the meaning of that form. These concepts are certainly not original. Similar conclusions have been reached by others in wholly different, and sometimes less laborious ways. The concepts are presented in the form of a list of categorical statements. They have been said before and hopefully, they will be said again.

1 Jerusalem is a city of panoramas. They are open and public, and commonly shared. Through them the awareness of the city's total form, and then of the meaning embodied in that form, is brought about. If Paris, with its street vistas radiating from key points, is a 'see-through city', then Jerusalem, with its panoramas, is a 'transparent city'.

2 Jerusalem's human character comes from its chequered history. The city is a mosaic of diverse communities. They are introverted, private, closed. Their built ensembles reflect their life.

3 Jerusalem is a city of visual harmony. The everyday life of its communities is expressed horizontally in a carpet of buildings and trees which follows the line of her hills.

4 Jerusalem is a city of visual and symbolic hierarchies. Structures of religious and public significance, marking the skyline, take their placement and their scale from the rhythms of the hills, and from the ordering principles of dominance and subdominance which obtain among them.

5 The Jerusalem skyline is thus the community's built expression of its scale of values.

6 Jerusalem is a city of human scale.

7 Jerusalem is a city of open spaces, following the topography, linked in sequence, leading ultimately to the Old City.

8 Jerusalem's landscape, with its delicate scale and textures, is of an extraordinary beauty.

9 The Old City of Jerusalem is a walled city, compact and clearly set off from its surroundings. It also forms, together with its landscape, an inseparable whole.

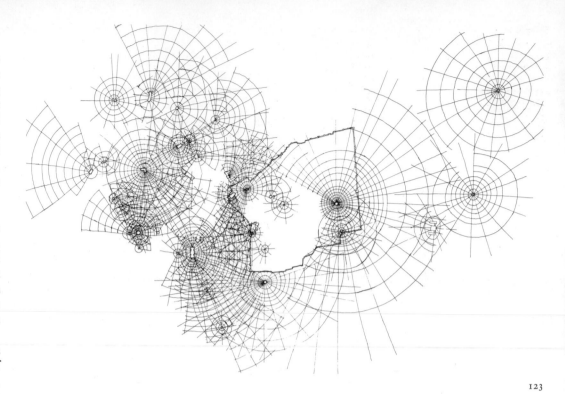

123

10 Jerusalem has been a sacred site for thousands of years. It is a holy city for three world religions. Its form is considered by many to be the physical expression of an ideal. As the capital of Israel, with the potentialities which that implies, Jerusalem also represents a great promise.

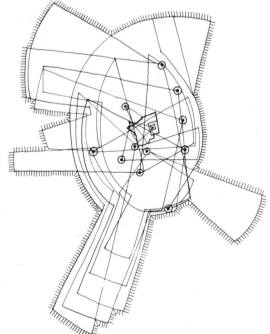

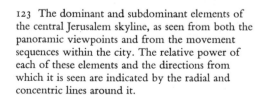

123 The dominant and subdominant elements of the central Jerusalem skyline, as seen from both the panoramic viewpoints and from the movement sequences within the city. The relative power of each of these elements and the directions from which it is seen are indicated by the radial and concentric lines around it.

124 Jerusalem, the Transparent City: a composite diagram of the major panoramic views in and around the Old City area.

124

125 The Old City of Jerusalem is a walled city, compact and clearly set off from its surroundings. It is surrounded on three sides by steep slopes; the topography suggests that the Damascus Gate (A) is the principal entrance to the Old City.

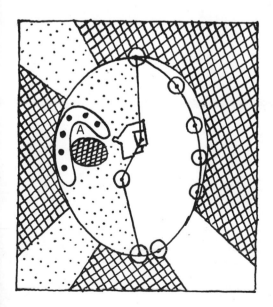

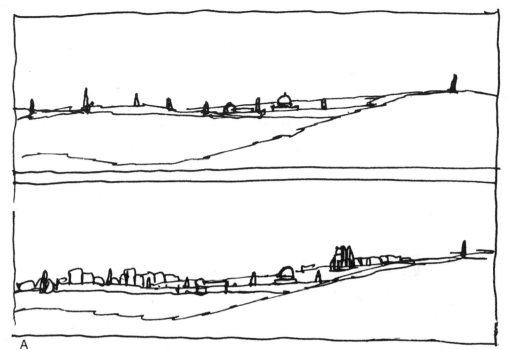

A

B

127

126 Diagrammatic map of the Old City's visual space. The spaces are enclosed by ridges on the west, south and east. There are major diagonal 'windows' to the Judeán hills to the north-east and south-west, and to the Judean Desert to the south-east. The visual structure of the area is particularly sensitive to buildings on the ridge at A.

127 A The view of the Old City from the south-east would be corroded by medium-scale contemporary structures; B Buildings on the crucial ridge at A in diagram 126, silhouetted in the afternoon sun, would overpower not only the Dome of the Rock but also the entire Old City.

# IV The real and true city of Jerusalem

*'I have set watchmen upon thy walls, O Jerusalem, which shall never hold their peace day nor night'*

THE SENSE THAT the city's reunification in 1967 had presented a once-in-a-lifetime chance was shared by Israelis with people the world over. Given Israel's talent and energy, with the vast resources of modern technology, and with the goodwill of half the world, there was the possibility that the building of Jerusalem could become the shining achievement of our age. Mayor Teddy Kollek's undoubtedly genuine desire to help fulfil this kind of hope led to the setting up of the Jerusalem Committee shortly after the city's reunification. The committee was a group of world-famous philosophers, historians, philanthropists, artists and architects, whose advice was to help guide the city's growth. At its first meeting in 1969 general issues were discussed, and in December 1970 a second meeting, this time of the town-planning sub-committee, was called together. At this meeting, the committee was presented with the Jerusalem Master Plan, the Old City area scheme, and a brief outline of the still unfinished Central Business District plan.

The Master Plan has briefly been described in Chapter II (page 54). It reflected the basic goals of the national and municipal governments. The plan had first of all been conceived in a national context. Jerusalem had been the capital of Israel since 1948, and with the city's

128 Key map of central Jerusalem showing the projects mentioned in this chapter. A the Jewish quarter; B the Alliance scheme; C the Plaza Hotel; D the Damascus Gate area; E the Jaffa Gate scheme; F Nikoforia; G Abu-Tor; H St John's Hospital; I the National Park; J Yemin Moshe; K Omaria; L the King David Hotel; M the Commodore Hotel; N Beit Ha'am; O Beit Midot.

reunification came the will to stamp it with the character of an Israeli, and primarily a Jewish city. In terms of official policy this involved the transfer of large government offices from Tel Aviv to Jerusalem, and a corresponding increase in the city's Israeli population. The Master Plan had not however proposed Jerusalem as the target for mass immigration from abroad. Nor did the proposed change in the city's demographic character imply that the rights of Jerusalem's Arab minority were to be ignored. In Israel's governing circles there seems to be a general agreement that the city's Arabs are to be treated fairly, as long as their legal rights do not conflict too sharply with what is felt to be the national interest. Certainly the Jerusalem Municipality under Mayor Kollek has gone to considerable lengths to ensure that the legal and human rights of its Arab citizens are respected.

From the local perspective, the Jerusalem Municipality saw the Master Plan as an instrument for promoting the city's economic growth. The Municipality, like nearly all city governments, is chronically in debt, and has compelling reasons for being so. The city has a high proportion of underprivileged Sephardic Jews (Jews from Arab-speaking countries). The *Sephardim* have the lowest incomes and the largest families in Jewish Jerusalem. Relatively low income is a general problem: since the city has little industry, employment is usually found in lower-paid service activities. As a result, the Municipality has a low tax-base, and high welfare costs. Social tensions, sometimes severe, already exist between *Sephardim* and

THE MAYOR
*It's sad*
*To be the Mayor of Jerusalem.*
*How can any man be the mayor of a city like that?*
*What can he do with her?*
*He will build, and build, and build.*

Amichai

129 The Jerusalem Master Plan. (See p.53.)

*Ashkenazim* (European Jews). The economic gap between Jews and Arabs may in the future produce similar, and more serious social tensions. All this points to the pressing need for improving employment opportunities, and for raising city revenues to provide improved educational and social service. The Master Plan, as well as other proposals, represents the Municipality's attempt to solve, in a rather indirect way, these urgent problems.

The Master Plan is a general and long-range strategy for the city's growth. It contains no detailed building proposals. It is a purely advisory document with no legal force. Yet the plan provoked a furious response among the members of the Jerusalem Committee.

## The Jerusalem Committee's Reaction to the Master Plan

At the date of writing, two years have passed since the Committee's meeting. Because of the swift pace of events over these two years, the 1970 session of the Jerusalem Committee now seems in many ways as remote as the Mameluke invasion. At a hastily called special session, closed to the public, the members of the Committee expressed their feelings about the plans to the Israeli authorities. Most of them were enraged by what they had seen. Some of them wept, others were nearly hysterical, and at least one was taken ill. The officials, who had expected the usual pat on the back given by such convocations of visiting firemen, were completely amazed. It had apparently never occurred to them that anyone would take a town plan so to heart.

The Jerusalem Committee's criticisms varied, and were not always consistent. Some members protested against the 'fake kitsch' of the Old City's Jewish Quarter reconstruction, some demanded more modernity, other more preservation; but the critics all agreed on one point: that the Jerusalem Master Plan, in its form, its content, and its spirit, was wholly inadequate to guide the building of the New Jerusalem, which they all sensed was at issue. Instead of an exemplary and visionary document, with principles that expressed man-

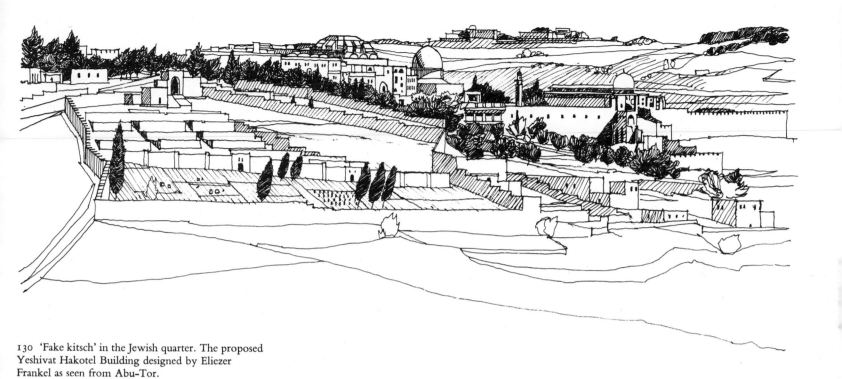

130 'Fake kitsch' in the Jewish quarter. The proposed Yeshivat Hakotel Building designed by Eliezer Frankel as seen from Abu-Tor.

kind's highest ideals, what they were given was a technically competent, conventional, rather outmoded plan, based upon the principles of the British Town and Country Planning Act, 1947. The Plan's form was criticized as being inadequate to its purpose; it was an old-fashioned coloured map without sufficiently clear principles and policies behind it to guide the city's growth properly. It proposed no effective mechanism to ensure its implementation; nor, with its hierarchic and purely deductive form, did it allow either for the process of feedback or for the democratic participation of the public. The plan's time-span, projecting growth forty years into the future, was considered too long, while its spatial context, Jerusalem and its immediate region, was held to be too limited, since this context ignored the need to co-ordinate the pattern of Jerusalem's growth with those of Haifa and Tel Aviv.

The major features of the plan's content, the proposed dense commercial core, served by a network of new arterial roads, and by an inner ring of motorways, as well as the unified and uniformly characterless quality of the new city, were all felt to be unnecessarily repeating well-known mistakes already made in other cities, and thus were strongly condemned as 'collective hara-kiri'.

But it was the spirit behind the plan which provoked the most and the bitterest criticism. The Jerusalem Master Plan was singled out as a particularly pernicious example of 'trend-planning', that value-free and permissive kind of planning which accepts present trends, such as rates of increase in motorization, projects these trends into the future, and tries then to accommodate them. The Jerusalem Committee strongly felt that Jerusalem's planning should be based upon a set of *principles* rather than *trends*, and that these principles might actually require that some present trends be decisively reversed. This demand came in turn from the

Committee's uneasy sense that nowhere in the Master Plan was there an attempt to define Jerusalem's special quality, nor to translate this special quality into generative principles which would guide the city's future growth, nor was there any assurance that this special quality would not be smothered in the rather hum-drum commercial and administrative city which the Master Plan had in mind.

And so the Master Plan was rejected by the Jerusalem Committee with the recommendation that it be completely revised, or 'restructured' as the Committee's unanimous final resolution put it. This criticism caused a public furor, both in Israel and abroad, and this furor has marked the beginning of a positive tendency: the active involvement of the public in the city's planning. In a way the Jerusalem Committee merely articulated a feeling which many Jerusalemites had sensed for some time, that the city's planning was on the wrong track.

## The Fate of the Master Plan

The Jerusalemites' uneasy feelings about their city's future were not caused by the Master Plan, of which they were virtually unaware. These feelings were provoked by specific projects which had already begun and by rumours of future, more extensive development. These projects were often more extreme than the Master Plan would have allowed. Even before the Jerusalem Committee's meeting, a series of *ad hoc* schemes promoted by both the Municipality and the Ministry of Housing had effectively cancelled out many of the Master Plan's proposals. The meeting of the Municipal Council at which the Master Plan's height limits for the commercial centre were presented illustrated the authorities' attitude toward its recommendations. The plan's proposals for city-wide and central area height limits were presented to the council. These entailed a general seven storey limit, with a maximum height of twelve storeys in the city centre. The Municipal Council accepted these recommendations, the planners were thanked, and left the meeting. The Council then got down to business and approved a speculative, government-backed scheme for the city centre consisting of a collection of eighteen- and twenty-storey office blocks.

This casual attitude toward formal town plans may alarm those accustomed to the more systematic procedures in at least some Western cities. To understand town-planning decisions in Jerusalem it should be pointed out that the authorities had seldom felt a great need for formal town-planning. Building had taken place organically: the vernacular of construction and the uniform use of Jerusalem stone had ensured an appropriateness and continuity to the city's growth. Planning problems seemed to take care of themselves. Formal town plans were a device imported from the West, and the need for them was not thoroughly grasped. Turkish law and practice better reflected the authorities' attitude: if the roof was up by morning, the building was legal. It should be further understood that before 1967, Jerusalem had not been plagued by excessive rates of growth. Indeed, the authorities' main problem had not been to control growth, but to promote it. Of course these Turkish procedures are no longer adequate to cope with large-scale technological development.

It is thus clear that the planning strategies, policies and decisions which will form the Jerusalem of the future are not to be found in the Master Plan, nor are they explicitly stated in any other official plans. At present, the

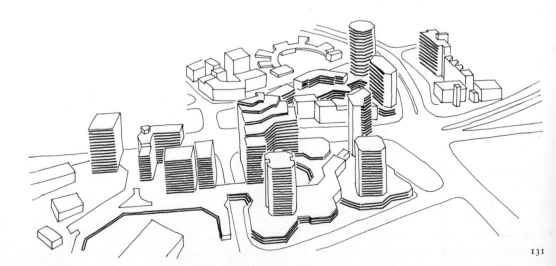

131 Aerial view of the Alliance scheme, approved despite the proposed height limits in the Master Plan.

131

process by which planning strategies are evolved, the priorities upon which they are based, and the policies and plans which implement them all seem to indicate that the great hopes for the building of Jerusalem, which arose at the time of the city's reunification, may never be realized.

## How planning works in Jerusalem

The process by which major planning decisions are arrived at in Jerusalem is in many ways similar to other cities. Peter Lennon's description of policies and building in his *Sunday Times* article 'Paris, bloody Paris' (November 1972), could have been written about Jerusalem. 'It was in no sense a conspiracy that big business took over to the exclusion of the needs of the ordinary citizen. It was the natural reaction of the financial giants of France, who found themselves with a government composed of men who had an automatic appreciation of their needs. In a smaller city, urban development projects which ignore the most elementary needs of the ordinary citizen – hardly any of the developments provide low-cost housing – have to be initiated with a certain caution for public opinion, or some politicians will be put on the spot and lose their votes. But because of the neutral, rubber stamp role that the Paris Municipal Council has been reduced to over the years, it has become impossible to fasten the blame on any particular politician or even party. So, in Claude Bourdet's expressive use of English, "self-service" was initiated. The developers and speculators served themselves to Paris.'

The planning decisions arrived at in this manner result in a series of arbitrary and isolated fiats. Each scheme is considered on its own merits. The only criterion by which these merits are measured is that of financial gain.

## Strategies

The city's physical form is also being strongly influenced by the dispute over strategy between the Jerusalem Municipality and the Ministry of Housing. The dispute is not about what, or how, or for whom to build, but rather where

to build. Oddly enough, both sides phrase their arguments in aesthetic and philosophical terms. The Ministry of Housing, in order to preserve Jerusalem's historic core, is removing pressure from it by building its housing estates at a respectful distance, in Jerusalem's surrounding hills. The Municipality, with its love for the landscape, proposes a compact city with a dense core, so as to prevent the surrounding hills from being despoiled. In addition to these sentimental considerations, the dispute also concerns some very practical issues.

The Jerusalem Municipality and the speculators, including the Israel Lands Authority which acts in effect as the governmental land speculator, are all advocates of a compact Jerusalem punctuated by high-rise luxury residential clusters and a dense, concentrated commercial core. Each party supports this concept since high density is felt to be in the financial interest of each of the proponents. In order to insure that all parties derive maximum financial benefit from high density, large areas of central Jerusalem have in effect been frozen by lack of planning, thus driving up land prices. This explains for instance why the Central Business District plan has remained for two years gathering dust on a shelf and has never been submitted for legal approval.

If the Municipality and its associates have an interest in patiently allowing pressures to build up in the centre of the city, the Ministry of Housing, with its reputation for swift action, and its taste for the *tabula rasa*, has gone out into Jerusalem's landscape, where it is building, as quickly as it possibly can, those middle- and upper-income blocks of flats, designed for Tel-Aviv, and faced with Jerusalem stone, in which it specializes. And so, because of the continuing dispute, undesirable effects which *both* parties wished to prevent are happening: Jerusalem's historic centre is being threatened by tremendous pressures, and the surrounding hills are being marred by insensitive building.

## Attitudes and Priorities

Underlying the processes and strategies which are shaping the city are a series of planning

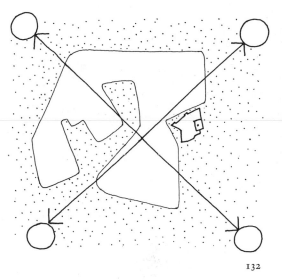

132

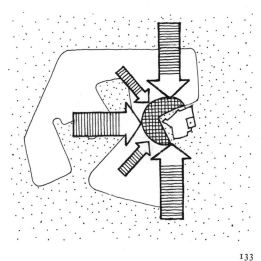

133

132 The Ministry of Housing's planning concept: housing estates placed at a respectful distance from the Old City on the hills surrounding Jerusalem.

133 The Jerusalem Municipality's planning concept: a compact Jerusalem concentrated around the Old City preserving the surrounding hills.

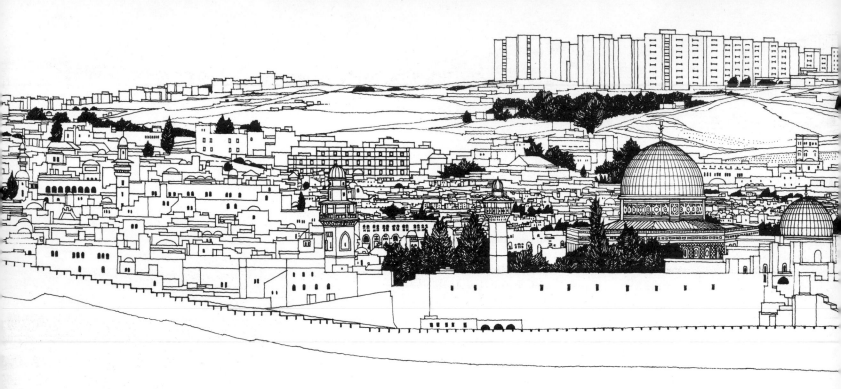

attitudes and priorities which motivate Jerusalem's decision-makers. First among the articles of faith is a familiar one, common to political and business leaders everywhere: economic growth is an unquestioned Good in itself, regardless of its consequences. Jerusalem therefore should become a large bustling commercial centre, with all the facilities and characteristics of a modern city. A certain philosophical attitude toward Jerusalem also seems to be involved in the decision-makers' priorities; a desire to dispense with all the tourist guidebook and picture postcard sentimentality, all of the romanticism and the religious hocus-pocus, and get down to business

134  The housing estate on French Hill seen from the Mount of Evil Counsel (Government House). Architect: Shmuel Shaked.

in a hardheaded and unemotional way to make Jerusalem into a normal city where ordinary people lead everyday lives. There is a characteristically Israeli tough-mindedness in this determination not to be impressed with vague sentiments. Another of the decision-makers' axioms is that the magnetism of Jerusalem's religious and historical heritage is a resource to be exploited intensively. Similarly, the beauty of her landscape and of her panoramic views are commodities to be sold in order to obtain foreign currency. Finally, it is axiomatic that immediate and often short-lived financial and political problems are to be solved by building permanent solutions. A temporary difficulty in the national balance of payments is immortalized in reinforced concrete and stone, changing forever the city's form. The panic produced by the Rogers peace plan in 1969

found its built expression in the housing estate which sits like a lead helmet on French Hill, above the Old City.

As mentioned in the discussion of the Master Plan, the basic governmental priorities which motivate planning decisions in Jerusalem involve the political and social unification of the city, and its economic expansion. The latter is to be achieved especially by making Jerusalem into a magnet for the minority of well-to-do new immigrants who can afford to pay for the luxury accommodation now being constructed. The governmental priority is that Jerusalem should attract, not great masses of immigrants, but large sums of foreign currency and great numbers of tourists. The goal is, of course, a favourable balance of payments. It should be noted that Israel's present situation in that respect is by no means desperate.

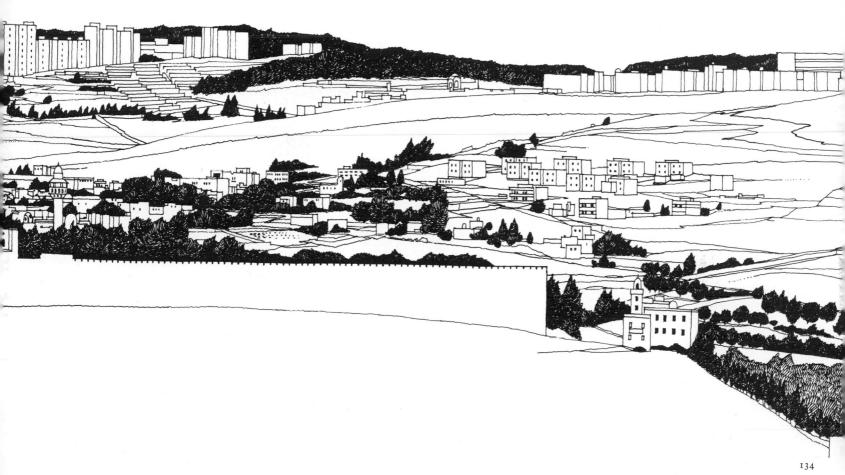

134

The decision-makers' strategies and priorities are implemented through a series of policies, which have never been publicly announced. Since the Jerusalem Municipality, the Government Ministries, and the speculative developers are not in the habit of issuing joint policy statements, the following list has been pieced together inductively from empirical data.

**Tourism**

The policy for developing tourism is standard the world over for promoting remote and undeveloped sites: foreign investment in hotels is encouraged by a series of public subsidies – public land (in Jerusalem's case, sometimes expropriated land) is sold at very favourable prices, low interest government loans pay for up to 70% of the land and building costs, direct cash payments on a per-tourist per-day basis

subsidize the hotels' operating costs, and tax-free profits are allowed to be taken out of the country without restriction. The fact that the investor pays less than half of the real costs of the project is felt to be justified by the foreign currency investment, by the additional foreign money brought by tourists, and by the employment in construction and tourist industries which the project provides. One could indeed argue that Jerusalem is not some remote beach in Spain; it is already a natural centre for tourism, and would therefore surely still be attractive to foreign investment without such overly-generous subsidies. But the Ministry of Tourism's policy is to promote extremely intensive development, regardless of cost.

The Ministry justifies this attitude by its table of statistics, which simply projects the present high growth rate in the city's tourism

into the future, producing the official vision of the New Jerusalem: in 1985, the city, by then with a population of about 500,000, will have to accommodate 6,000,000 tourists. The procedure of projecting current trends far into the future is fallacious but even in the unlikely event that the forecast were statistically accurate, it is clear that it does not necessarily have to be accommodated and encouraged; it can equally well be prevented.

The way in which specific projects are decided upon and in which sites are chosen is less scientific. Ministerial officials receive word that a foreign investor is in town, who is interested in building a large luxury hotel. The man is invited to lunch, and after they have been assured to their satisfaction that he is actually prepared to build a mammoth luxury hotel just like those in Miami Beach, the

93

officials take the man for a little drive around the city. He is shown four or five of the city's breathtaking panoramic views, all on public open space, and is then asked which he would prefer. He chooses, the deal is sealed, and shortly thereafter the legal planning committees make their mark on the official document.

## Housing Policy

The housing policy concerned with providing luxury accommodation for wealthy new immigrants follows roughly similar lines. Its promoters are the Ministries of Finance and Housing, along with private development firms. The policy has the endorsement of the municipal authorities, as they feel that new residents are necessary to help solve the city's social and financial problems. The money that wealthy immigrants spend in Jerusalem will, by the mechanism of 'trickle-down' economics, ultimately reach the poor, and the taxes which they pay will prop up the Municipality's sagging finances. The wealthy will also help the poor 'by giving a lot of money to charity', in the words of one developer. But the general public has to pay a heavy price for the privilege of having such generous neighbours. Their luxury tower blocks, sited on public open space, or even in public parks, provide their inhabitants with some of Jerusalem's most magnificent views, but of course block them for everyone else. These buildings break Jerusalem's horizontal skyline, serving as harsh symbols of social inequality and governmental favouritism. To attract these new wealthy residents, the government allows them considerable tax relief, duty-free import privileges, and until very recently low-interest housing loans. The immigrants who purchase accommodation in an 'apartment hotel' receive, as a reward for being absentee landlords, further privileges: a five-year exemption from income tax, one half the normal corporation tax rate, free transfer of currency out of the country, exemption from estate duty, property tax levied at one-third the normal rate, and depreciation deductions at double the normal rate.

## Open Space and Public Land Policy

The open space policies of the Municipality and the Israel Lands Authority demonstrate one of the most disturbing tendencies in the city's development. To appreciate its importance it should be recalled that the development of an interconnected sequence of open spaces based on Jerusalem's topography and upon her panoramic views was a key feature of most of the city's statutory plans. It should also be emphasized that the city has a deficiency of parks and public open spaces. According to generally recognized international standards, Jerusalem has less than half of the parkland and open space required for a city of her population. The amount of open space in Jerusalem which has actually been made into parkland is extremely small, representing about one-tenth of her needs. Although the city is growing rapidly, no co-ordinated policy to expand her parkland correspondingly has been developed. On the contrary, her present insufficient stock of public open space is being gradually reduced by a series of *ad hoc* decisions which allow hotels and luxury flats to be built on public open space, or on land zoned for community facilities. In one case the decision-makers have really outdone themselves by allowing a luxury apartment hotel, the Plaza, to be built within the central municipal park.

While the Municipal Council allows speculative development to eat away the city's parks and open spaces, the Israel Lands Authority quietly sits on its holdings. Large areas of open space around the Old City which were zoned for public parkland in virtually all of the city's plans are being patiently held by the Lands

135 The Plaza in the Park. Architect: Mote Ben Chorin.

136 Location plan of the Plaza Hotel (A) in Independence Park.

137 Public parks in central Jerusalem.

138 Parks and gardens in central London at the same scale.

135

136

137

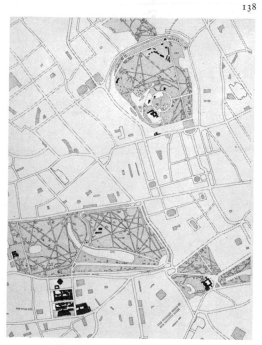

138

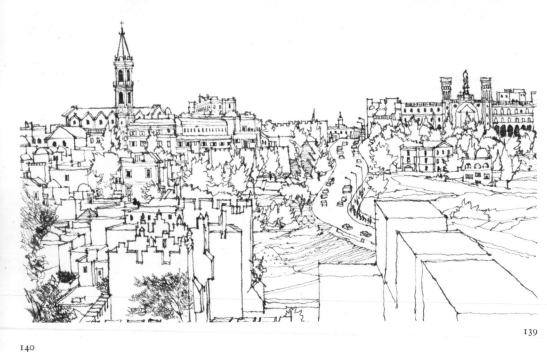

139 View of the Damascus Gate area from the Old City wall.

140 One of many plans proposing a park outside the Damascus Gate. (Numbers of storeys indicated.)

141 Map of rubbish dumps around the Old City. A Mount Scopus; B the Damascus Gate area; C Omaria; D Nikoforia; E Abu-Tor; F the Mount of Evil Counsel.

142 Diagrammatic section looking east to the proposed park in front of the Damascus Gate.

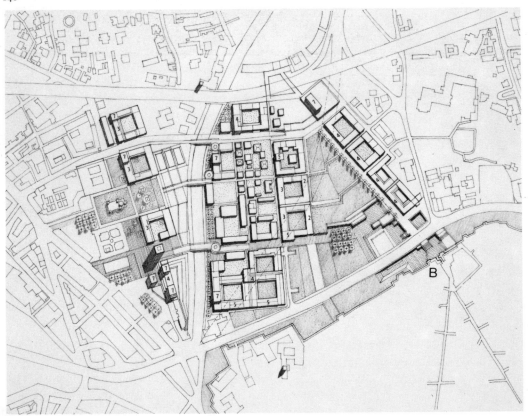

140

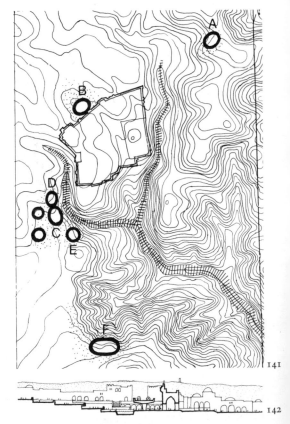

141

142

Authority until the value has risen sufficiently to justify their sale for hotels and villas. To make sure that the public does not become accustomed to using these tracts of land as if they were parks, and to insure that the views from them will not be missed when they are eventually blocked by luxury housing, the Lands Authority, with the co-operation of the Municipality, has instituted a programme of rubbish dumping on these sites. Dump-trucks, often under municipal contract, illegally deposit the refuse from construction sites on some of the most beautiful areas of the Old City's landscape. The projects from which this refuse comes are usually the luxury hotels and flats, the social housing for the wealthy in which the government and the Municipality specialize. Perhaps the most outrageous of these actions is now occurring immediately outside the Damascus Gate of the Old City. The historic Tyropean valley is being filled with thousands of tons of rubbish, guaranteeing that several plans drawn up for making the valley into a public park will never be realized. The area will instead become a parking lot and then undoubtedly a hotel site. The Municipal Beautification Department, who have the specific task of controlling the dumping of rubbish, have done nothing to stop these actions.

## High Building Policy

Except for those instances in which its bull-dozers and dump-trucks are implementing the Municipal Landscape Plan for the Old City, the city government does not normally take the initiative in planning matters. It usually waits patiently for others to make the first move. The city's high building policy is an illustration. Although the city has never officially stated its policy for high buildings, and although it has approved a great number of them without proper planning guidelines, there is an implicit policy behind its actions.

The Municipality wants first of all to attract the heavy construction industry to Jerusalem to provide employment and tax revenue. The Israeli building industry has recently invested a large amount of capital in high-rise construction equipment, much of it French, produced by the same engineering firms who are making possible the rebuilding of Paris. This equipment must be put to use. Jerusalem, with its dilapidated central area, and its housing shortage, seems to the authorities to be the ideal place to do it. Secondly, government and municipal officials generally share a sense of shame about Jerusalem: she does not look imposing enough to be the capital of Israel. They of course realize that Jerusalem can probably never rival Manhattan. So they have set their sights a bit lower. Their dream of Jerusalem is a sort of copy of Kansas City.

But even more fundamental than any aesthetic vision is what the Municipality considers to be its extremely shrewd financial strategy. This strategy clearly dictates the use of high-rise construction for the municipally-promoted luxury housing projects and hotels. Since there are only a limited number of beautiful views in Jerusalem, each should be exploited to its fullest. It is also because of this strategy that the city has not formulated clear guidelines and height limits to govern the siting of high building projects, and has allowed the proposed new legal plan for the central business district to gather dust on a shelf for two years. The moment there were new legal plans for the centre with strictly enforced height and density limits, property speculation would cease and land values would more or less adjust themselves to the realities of supply and demand, assuming the plan provided reasonable accommodation for facilities needed in the centre. The Municipality is not interested in accommodating the real pressures for growth in the central area. It is working instead to create artificial pressures. The city began this process by approving a few high-rise schemes judiciously scattered about the central area, and by subsidizing the construction of the first one. This created the expectation of further high-density projects throughout the centre, and land prices began to skyrocket. Low- and medium-density projects, which were within the limits of the existing 1959 legal plan, were

no longer economically feasible. High density was required to provide a reasonable return on the developer's investment. To obtain permission for additional densities, the developer makes a direct cash payment to the city, in the form of a betterment tax. Thus, by the sly device of not announcing a high building policy, and not approving a new legal plan for the centre, the municipal officials have found a way of obtaining badly needed municipal revenue.

It must be emphasized that in Jerusalem high building projects do not reflect the need for accommodation in the central area, but are wholly the result of land prices which have been artificially inflated through speculation. That these projects do not correspond to the actual market demands for floor space in the city centre is illustrated by the fact that Jerusalem's only high-rise office block, built by a private developer, had finally to be filled with municipal and government offices since no-one else could afford the high rents. (Because of high land costs and because a high building costs more to build per square foot than a low one, its rents are higher.) The speculators are of course quite satisfied with the process. If no-one else is prepared to rent the space, governmental clients will come to their rescue. If the high-rise projects already approved for the centre area are finally built, the authorities will have quite a bit of floor space to fill, since surveys done by the planning team for the Central Business District show that the great demand in the central area is for commercial accommodation at ground and first floor level, and not for expensive office space. One of the projects alone would accommodate the entire office space demand for all of central Jerusalem for the next fifteen years.

The city's policy of encouraging speculation not only fails to realize its own short-sighted goals; it is also, in a larger context, highly irresponsible. The simple fact is that the city can afford to build only a very small part of the new road system which its proposed high-density commercial centre will require. The few roads which can be built will slice through the existing fabric of the city, and will be

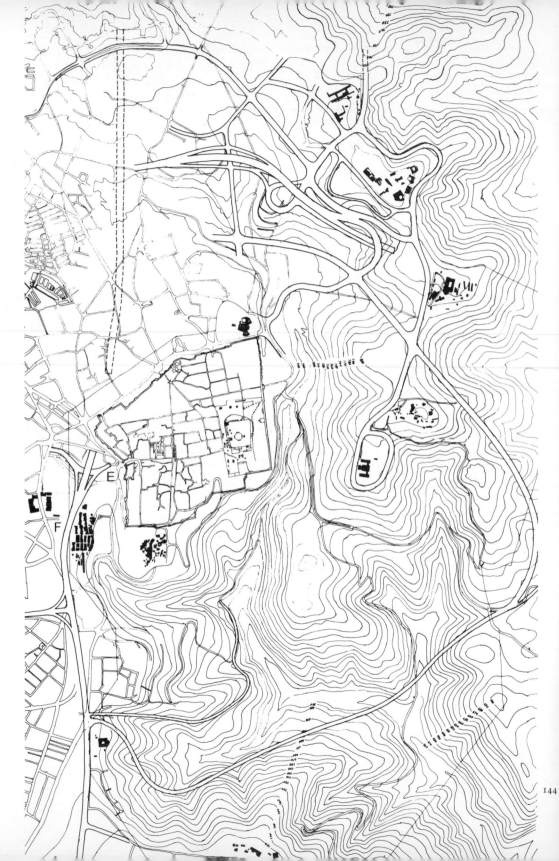

143 Suggested design for the Central City Park
at Nikoforia (F).

144 Road schemes being studied and designed in
the Old City area. The scheme for a road leading
to the Jaffa Gate development at E and bisecting
the Nikoforia area at F has strong municipal backing.
Some of the roads in the upper portion of the site
are now under construction.

extremely expensive. Certainly the prices paid by the developers to the city for increased densities will never pay for these roads, nor will these payments ever compensate the city and its citizens for social costs arising from the excessive traffic congestion and environmental deterioration which these projects will inevitably bring.

## Road Policy

The building of roads holds a special fascination for municipal and government officials in Jerusalem, as it does for their colleagues throughout the world. 'It is an elementary planetary rule of politics that there is nothing like a really good road to make politicians and their constituents happy. There are surveys to be made, contracts to be let, jobs to hand out, land to be bought and sold, gas station and motel concessions to be awarded, and trees to be knocked down in the thousands. Isn't it also an elementary rule that roads mean development and progress?' (Claire Stirling in the *International Herald Tribune*, 15 November 1972). But the Municipality cannot afford to build all of the roads it needs, or would like.

Because of the high-density projects already approved, and because the officials in Jerusalem can hardly be expected to take steps to limit the use of private cars, some new roads must be built. For economic reasons these will be sited wherever possible on public open space and in parks. Since the Old City area is the largest reserve of open space near the centre, its landscape has become one of the road planner's favourite sites; it is felt to be particularly suitable for giant interchanges. But because of strong public criticism of these schemes, the municipal authorities have recently announced that no road of more than four lanes will be allowed in the vicinity of the Old City. Previously, rights of way of up to eight lanes had been proposed for the area. Four-lane roads are for the most part inconceivable in the delicate textures and scale of the Old City's landscape; yet the public is supposed to be grateful for the reduction of a hideous proposal to one that is merely grotesque.

The public can be assured that the roads proposed for the Old City area will be built, unless a firm policy is demanded which entirely prohibits them. In particular, one road which is considered vitally necessary to provide access to a proposed giant commercial centre and parking garage just outside the Jaffa Gate will bisect an area opposite the Old City walls which has long been zoned to become the city's main park. The commercial centre is one of the Municipality's pet projects, and is kept strictly secret. The project is in an advanced stage of detailed planning, and the dump-trucks have been easing the proposed parkland into its new role by depositing heaps of rubbish upon it.

## Aesthetic Policies

The contention that aesthetic values in architecture and town-planning are matters of subjective taste is basic to official policy. Since aesthetic restrictions have no objective basis, the authorities are extremely reluctant to subject a developer's plans to architectural limitations which might entail additional costs. For the same reason, the architect's right of self-expression is not to be infringed. But as the examination of the city's planning history has shown, certain of Jerusalem's architectural principles are not wholly subjective.

There is, however, one aesthetic rule which is strictly enforced and that is the requirement that all buildings in Jerusalem be faced in natural stone. Having required this of the developers, the authorities feel that they have fulfilled the demands of Architectural Beauty. The way in which they apply the rule demonstrates a complete lack of understanding of its purpose. The point of the stone rule is to insure that individual buildings blend in with their neighbours, and that the whole ensemble fits in with the landscape. A twenty-four storey tower block faced with Jerusalem stone is an obvious and absurd contradiction.

In terms of planning priorities aesthetic values are considered to be merely a sentimental and expensive luxury which must give way to what are considered to be the realities of economics and politics. This official attitude was clearly expressed when the Master Plan's list of buildings for preservation was presented to the city authorities. After careful research, the plan listed five thousand buildings in the city which merited preservation for historical, religious or architectural reasons. The entire list was thrown out, the reason given being that it would be impossible to build the city if so much of it had to be preserved. As a result, there are no listed buildings in Jerusalem.

## Approval of Plans: Legal Procedures

Based on these strategies, priorities and policies, the major plans and projects which determine the form of the city are drawn up. The plans are, in most cases, submitted to the statutory town-planning committees for their legal approval before being carried out. The Committees tend to rubber-stamp projects which have high level backing. It is worthwhile briefly to examine the process by which plans receive legal approval, since a strengthening of statutory review procedures and an expansion of the public's legal rights are essential to improving Jerusalem's town-planning situation.

The legal procedures of town-planning in Jerusalem are derived from British Mandatory law and practice, modified by the Israeli planning law of 1965. The final power of decision in town-planning matters, excepting appeals, rests with the District Town-planning Commission, composed of civil-service appointees representing those government ministries with a direct interest in town-planning – Transport, Housing, Defence, etc. – and headed by the Ministry of the Interior, nominally in charge of planning at the national level. Representatives of the Jerusalem Municipality and of the Architects' Society sit on the Commission, as does a professional architect who heads the Commission's technical staff, and who for five lonely years has fought a courageous holding action against political blindness and speculative greed.

The Jerusalem Municipal Council's building and planning sub-committee is one step below the District Town-planning Commission in its jurisdiction. The Municipal Council's members are named by their respective political parties, chosen according to Israel's system of indirect elections. The municipal town-planning sub-committee deals with the day-to-day business of issuing building permits, which, so long as they conform with the zoning law, need not be passed on to the District Commission. All requests for permission to deviate from the zoning law, as well as all new town plans, are referred, with the Municipal Council's recommendations, to the District Commission for final decision. The City Engineer's Department of the Jerusalem Municipality acts as technical advisory staff to the politicians of the Municipal Council. It should be emphasized that the City Engineers Department, with all its shortcomings, faces its enormous responsibilities with insufficient staff, overworked and underpaid, and that in spite of these difficulties, the department is performing a vital task, and provides the city with a useful service. The villains in the story of Jerusalem's town planning are not to be found among its municipal employees.

## The Role of the Public

The legal procedures do not provide for public hearings. Instead, public participation in planning is allowed for, in a rudimentary form, by the deposition procedure inherited from the British Mandate. Under British rule, this procedure bore witness to that residual sense of fairness that allowed even colonial subjects the right to object to a town-planning scheme, even if their objections were often disregarded. The way in which the Israeli Government administers these procedures virtually ensures that the public will not be able to interfere with the business of planning. According to the law, any new town-planning scheme or any change to an existing legal town plan, after receiving approval from the authorities, must be deposited with the District Commission, and made available for public inspection. Anyone who considers himself aggrieved by the plan may present his objection to the District Commission. Since deposition occurs at the end of the planning process, the chance of the Local and District Commissions reversing what are in effect final decisions is slight.

Moreover, the method of notification and the form in which plans are presented to the public make it unlikely that a cogent objection can be made.

A small notice, identifying the plan only by its code number on the city's official Block and Parcel map, appears in the legal section of the daily newspapers. Those fortunate to possess a complete set of the city's Block and Parcel maps will be able to locate the project, but still not identify it. If, finally, anyone is lucky or clever enough to discover what site and what project is referred to in the legal notice, he may then proceed to the District Town-planning Commission, where he will be allowed to examine a coloured piece of paper, accompanied by a table of notes and figures. From this sort of information, it is extremely difficult for a layman, or even for an architect, to gain an adequate impression of what is actually being proposed, and what, if anything, should be objected to. The few objections which manage to pass through this filtering process are invariably dismissed by the Commission, unless substantive legal points are involved. In a few dramatic instances, objections based on town-planning and aesthetic arguments have been accepted by the Commission. These were, however, 'inside' objections, based upon the actual plans of a proposed scheme, which are normally not made available to the general public.

The hearing of public objections represents only a minor part of the District Town-planning Commission's work. For the most part, the Commission's time is spent in evaluating applications for *ad hoc* changes to the city's existing legal town plan. The major portion of these applications result from the planning policies outlined previously, and are usually approved. By permitting *ad hoc* changes at the insistence of higher authorities, the Commission has allowed the substance and spirit of Jerusalem's 1959 legal plan to be completely eroded.

### The Official Planners: The Urban Planning Unit

Recognizing the need for a new plan to replace the 1959 law, and for a general reorganization of planning procedures, a municipal councillor, Mr Meron Benvenisti, was able to persuade the Municipality, still reeling under the shock of the Jerusalem Committee's criticism, that a team of professional town-planners should be formed as the nucleus of a new Municipal Town-planning Department. The founding of the Urban Planning Unit under Mr Benvenisti's guidance represented a radical change in municipal procedure: previously the Municipality had farmed out the preparation of town-planning schemes to private firms. The new Urban Planning Unit, of which the present writer was for one year a member, set itself four basic tasks: to prepare a new legal plan for Jerusalem which would replace the sadly riddled 1959 plan; to advise the Municipal Town-planning Committee on matters of architecture and town-planning, particularly for the Old City area, and to do the Committee's homework so that it might be able to make intelligent decisions; to co-ordinate the work of the various public and private groups which were preparing plans for specific areas of the city; and finally to find out what had actually been approved over the last few years, and what, if anything, could be done about it. It was this final task which, during the planning unit's first year, absorbed most of its time and effort.

For more than a year, the unit operated without a direct administrative leader. Members of the unit were allowed, or allowed themselves, considerable freedom in their work. Key to the unit's collectively worked out strategy was the involvement of the public in planning issues. It is to be hoped that this tendency will continue under the new co-leadership of Jerusalem's town-planning, headed by Professor Nathaniel Litchfield and the City Engineer, Mr Amikam Yafeh.

The Urban Planning Unit's evaluation of the patchwork of public and private plans which it had inherited pointed to the need for an even more radical reorganization of planning procedures than had already taken place. It also became clear that most of the plans and policies which the authorities were promoting in fact made proper town-planning impossible, and therefore had to be reversed or eliminated. In order to understand what the future may hold in store for Jerusalem, the plans and projects with which the Urban Unit had to deal should be examined.

## The Central Business District Plan

The plan for the Central Business District, done by a team headed by David Best and Gilbert Weil, was assigned the task of working out the implications of the Master Plan's concept of a concentrated commercial core, and translating the result into a legal plan replacing the 1959 scheme.

Upon investigation, it was discovered that the central area densities proposed by the Master Plan were too high and that most of the Master Plan's central area road system was not feasible for environmental or economic reasons. As was mentioned earlier, the planning team found that high-rise office blocks did not answer the centre's real need for more commercial floor space. High-rise projects would also have the effect of producing 'peripheral blight'. The expectation of further high density projects in the area would tend to freeze improvement and renovation of existing commercial properties, since the owners were awaiting demolition and new construction. Thus the centre would become even more dilapidated than it already was. The planning team also found that the total expected increase in central area floor space over the next fifteen years could be accommodated in four- to seven-storey structures, built upon only those sites now vacant or open for redevelopment within the centre. It was therefore clear that high-rise projects were not needed. But even seven-storey buildings would not solve the

146

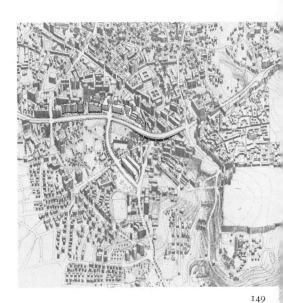

147

148

149

147 Planning studies indicate that if the shaded areas were developed with buildings of 4 to 7 storeys, the demand for central area floor space for the next 15 years could be accommodated.

148 A system of parks and pedestrian connections for the central area suggested by the CBD planners.

145 Isometric view of central Jerusalem.

146 Panoramic view of the Central Business District from Independence Park.

149 Isometric view of the Master Plan's proposed 'Central Boulevard' in Independence Park.

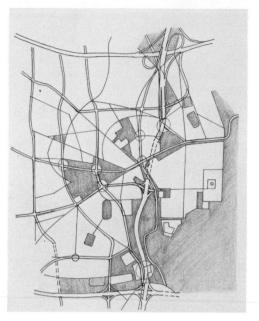

150     151     152

150 Open spaces and the connections between them based on the topography movement sequences and key viewpoints.

151 The Master Plan road network for central Jerusalem.

152 The open space system of central Jerusalem after the road system.

problem of ground- and first-floor accommodation needed for commercial activities.

Because the limited size of the Master Plan's concentrated centre could not answer this need, it was recommended that sub-centres, or expanded neighbourhood commercial facilities, be developed at an early date. This would also reduce the need for new roads in the area. For all of these reasons, lower densities than those of the Master Plan or of the *ad hoc* projects were recommended.

At an early stage in the study a sketch proposal for a high building policy was made, suggesting the placement of towers at intervals which would continue the rhythms of the dominant buildings in the Old City area. This scheme had to be discarded, since it was not legally possible to 'spot zone' sites for high buildings on a purely aesthetic basis; and more important, because the scale of office blocks was far too large to fit into the rhythms of the Old City's skyline.

The plan made other more positive proposals which included a large pedestrian precinct in the city's shopping core, an area-wide open space system with expanded parks and gardens, a pedestrian system which linked the parks with the existing street pattern, a series of views to be preserved, areas for preservation, and height limits for the entire central area of Jerusalem. That these recommendations and proposals contradicted some of the Master Plan's concepts did not unduly worry the authorities. But that the new plan also opposed the procedure of *ad hoc* high density schemes, and put stress upon parks and open spaces, view preservation and height limits, proved fatal for the plan. It was certainly one of the most serious pieces of work that Jerusalem town-planning has seen, and for that reason it has been ignored by the authorities who commissioned it.

## The Old City Plan

The 1970 Outline Plan for the Old City and its Environs by Arieh and Eldar Sharon and David Anatol Brutzkus also began as a serious piece of work, solidly within Jerusalem's town-planning tradition. The plan recognized the basic concept of Maclean's 1918 scheme, further elaborated by Rau in 1948, that the Old City's visual space was the 'harbour of Jerusalem', the place where the edge of the Jerusalem plateau, the 'green belt' penetrates to the very heart of the city. Conversely it is the place where the city's centre opens out dramatically to the desert. The importance of maintaining the integrity of the Old City's visual space was recognized as vital, since Jerusalem's other open spaces were and are being rapidly filled in. In its first versions, the plan also recognized the inherent logic of the existing edges of development in the Old City area. The boundaries of the built-up areas within the site are for the most part natural ones. Outside them land is generally unsuited for ordinary construction: slopes are very steep, soils and foundation conditions are

153 Zoning map of the Old City and its environs showing extensive hotel and residential developments (outlined areas) on the southern portion of the site.

154 The finally approved version of the Old City zoning map with the southern developments deleted.

155 A view of the Mount of Evil Counsel from Mount Zion. In spite of its much publicized decision to keep this area open, the Municipal Council is promoting an extensive private speculative development here—in spite also of the Mayor's opposition. The project, consisting of 8-storey flats, a 250-room hotel, and a building 200 metres long, has been designed by architect Resnik, designer of the King David Annexe, and the St John's Hotel. Resnik is chairman of the Jerusalem Architects' and Engineers' Association. The current project has begun with the illegal bulldozing of an access road across the face of the Mount of Evil Counsel. The project's legal adviser is Advocate Joseph Kokia, ex-Director General of the Ministry of Justice, who is also counsel for the St John's project, site of illegal demolition.

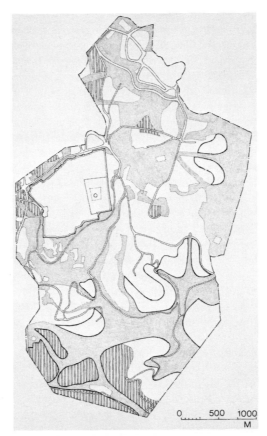

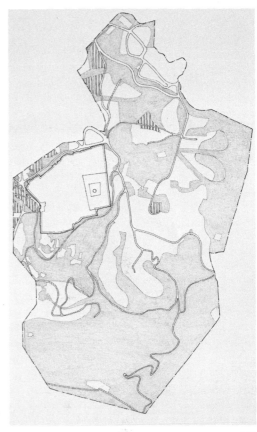

153

154

155

poor, as are exposures to the desert sun and wind. These realities were ignored mid-way in the planning process when the authorities decided for political and economic reasons to encourage the building of luxury villas and hotels over large portions of the site. Population figures were arbitrarily chosen: suddenly the Old City's landscape would have to accommodate three times the number of people which the Master Plan had proposed for it. Great numbers of hotels were to be sited on the southern rim of the Old City basin. The planners bravely tried to make the best of a bad situation, suggesting that the hotel's massive hulks would not really be seen, as they would be 'swallowed in shadows' during most of the day. The financial motive behind the decision were clear: the hotels and villas, in a matchless landscape, would command what many people consider to be the most magnificent views on earth. Politically the area seemed to be an ideal place for satisfying both Jewish and Arab housing needs; although those portions of the site slated for Arab housing would undoubtedly be acquired by speculators, and if the natives

105

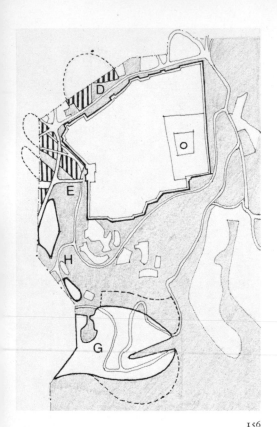

of these new villages spoke Arabic, it would be with a Brooklyn accent. Fortunately, strong objections were made to these proposals, both by the public and, decisively, by Mayor Teddy Kollek. The additions were removed, and the plan was legally approved, more or less as originally intended. It lacked a road system, since the planners could not accept the Master Plan's road system, and it had no clear architectural guidelines, but still it was better than no plan at all.

Unfortunately, upon closer examination there are some disturbing features about the final version of the plan. For anyone who is concerned about the beauty, integrity and meaning of the Old City and its landscape, the plan, and the way it is being interpreted by the authorities should give cause for very serious concern. First of all, there are vaguely-defined 'special planning areas' outside the Jaffa and Damascus Gates. The actual status of these plans is unknown, but they undoubtedly involve large commercial developments immediately outside both gates, with vast car parks, served by large roads. Both plans have already been mentioned (see pages 97 and 99) and it should be recalled that the Damascus Gate scheme is apparently already under way with the Municipal Landscape Specialists obliterating the Tyropean Valley. These intensive developments will have the effect of 'exploding' the Old City, changing its character from a primarily residential community to a commercial operation – a kind of religious Disneyland.

A second cause for concern is the absence from the plan of a series of maps which were originally intended by the planners as essential supplements to the basic zoning map. These were vital and conscientiously prepared maps showing the religious, historical and architectural monuments to be preserved in the Old City, the views to be protected in the city and the landscape, and the key portions of the site to be listed as nature preserves. These are essential parts of the plan, and their absence from the finally approved version means that there is no legally ensured protection of the Old City's monuments, or of its landscape.

156

156  Detailed map of the Old City and its immediate surroundings ('special planning areas' shown by vertical shading). D The Damascus Gate; E the Jaffa Gate; H St John's Hospital; G Abu-Tor.

157

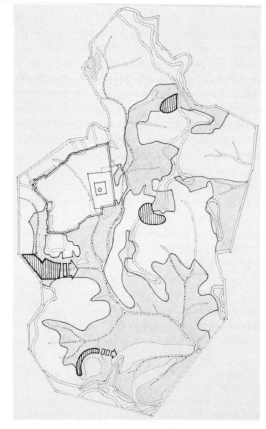

158

Certainly, the Dome of the Rock is in no danger, but many lesser buildings may be threatened, and the landscape itself, the matchless, delicate poignant landscape, the 'joy of the whole earth', is utterly without defence and is today being randomly bulldozed throughout its length and breadth.

## Abu-Tor

A third cause for concern is the plan for Abu-Tor, a detail plan for an area within the boundaries of the Old City scheme. The village of Abu-Tor, just to the south of the Old City, is sited on a hill which faces Mount Zion from across the Valley of Hell. Abu-Tor is visually and, so it seems, financially one of the key areas within the Old City basin. A detailed legal plan commissioned by the Municipality, supposedly developed according to the guidelines of the Old City area plan, has been produced by a firm of private architects. The architects' aesthetic vision shows a degree of harmony with the developers' profit chart which is unusual even for Jerusalem. They have proposed a new, modernized and much expanded version of Abu-Tor. It is a version in which blocks of super-luxury flats, taking advanatage of the marvellous view, elbow aside their older, smaller neighbours. It is a version in which new roads, certainly courageous works of highway engineering in such a recalcitrant landscape, guarantee smooth and easy access for the new residents. Although the

159

160

157  This map of buildings and areas to be preserved in the Old City was deleted from the legally approved zoning map.

158  The landscape- and view-preservation map was also deleted. The shaded area indicated nature reserves. The hatched portions are sites currently being bulldozed.

159  View from the Valley of Hell (Gehenna) to the Jaffa Gate, site of a large proposed commercial development. Architects: Arieh and Eldar Sharon.

160  An ensemble of buildings in the Old City which would have been protected by the map 157.

107

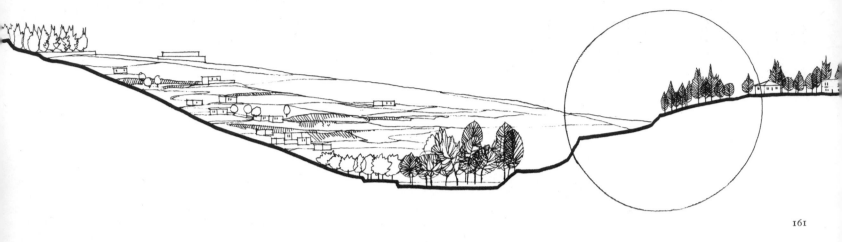

161 Section through Mount Zion, the Valley of
Gehenna and Abu-Tor looking east.

161

162 View of Abu-Tor from Mount Zion. The
dominant buildings centre and right are St John's
Hospital.

162

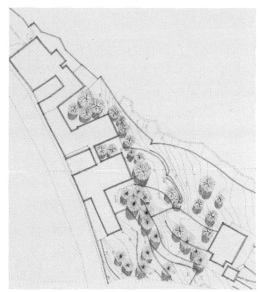

163

164

Master Plan proposed that Abu-Tor's population remain at about its present level of five thousand persons, with new construction only serving to thin out existing over-crowding; although the more expansionist Old City area plan envisaged seven thousand residents, the new detailed town plan provides for ten thousand residents, a number apparently derived from a careful study of the developers' account books. The area into which these new residents will expand with their luxury flats and new roads is precisely that area which a few months before was saved by the municipal authorities from the developers (see above, page 104) and designated as public open space, inviolable forever. It goes without saying that the Abu-Tor scheme has the support of the municipal officials.

**St John's**

The case of the St John's buildings illustrates how the legal provisions of the Old City area plan are being enforced. The buildings once housed the finest eye hospital in the Middle East, but since 1948 they have been vacant. St John's was to be preserved, renovated, and put to public use, according to the Master Plan, Central Business District plan, and the first version of the Old City plan. The site itself is traditionally considered by Christians to be the location of Armageddon, the final world-struggle between the forces of Good and Evil. The residents of Jewish Jerusalem have always considered the buildings beautiful and expressive. Unperturbed by all this, the Israel Lands Authority sold the buildings and their site, three acres of fine trees, to a foreign investor with the intention of demolishing the buildings and most of the trees, and replacing them with a luxury hotel whose swimming pool and discotheque would overlook the Valley of Hell. The authors of the Old City plan were compelled to accept this change of zoning, or see their entire plan thrown out. The developer became impatient after encountering delays in obtaining a building permit. To speed up the process, he began knocking down the existing buildings without obtaining a demolition permit, in violation of strict regulations in the Old City plan. The developer was served with a total of five court orders to cease, but he continued demolition and was

163 View of Abu-Tor from the Mount of Olives. A block of luxury flats and an apartment hotel stand out from the texture of buildings and trees and break the skyline. Small changes in scale have a great effect in Jerusalem.

164 Site plan of St John's Hospital. Most of the buildings, terraces and trees were to be destroyed to accommodate a luxury hotel.

165 View of St John's Hospital showing the effects of the developers' illegal demolition.

never prosecuted for what had become not merely a planning violation, but contempt of court.

The legal mechanisms of the Old City plan have no teeth because of official indifference, but the non-legal plans for the area are being forcefully carried out. Chief among these plans is the National Park scheme which is being implemented within the area of the Old City plan, but outside its jurisdiction. The major portion of the national park plan is being built without having been reviewed by the statutory planning committees, or by the municipal planning staff. The park occupies the steep slopes and the bottom of the Valley of Hell. Flatter and more accessible areas which adjoin the park are being closed to the public by projects such as St John's and the luxury housing proposed by the Abu-Tor plan. Narrow and difficult to reach, the park will serve primarily as a decorative feature to be seen from above rather than as a functioning part of a city park system. Because adjacent areas more appropriate for park use are being closed by private development, and because in other parts of the city open spaces and even parks are being reduced and built upon, the Municipality is attempting to compensate for these losses by devoting a kind of intensive fury to the building of the National Park. It is imperative that the work being done on the park be highly visible; the bulldozers chugging around the Old City give the officials something to point to when accused of doing nothing for the beauty of the city. The design of the park completely ignores the powerful simplicity and clarity of the Old City's relation to its landscape. Jerusalem's rock terraces and vegetation are being erased, and her ancient aqueduct is being blotted out by boulders randomly placed to create a kind of Cecil B. de Mille biblical set which completely negates the strict topographical, geologic, and historic givens of the site.

### Yemin Moshe

The case of Yemin Moshe illustrates how the authorities intend to raise the city's economic base and improve its population composition, and at whose expense this is to be done. Yemin Moshe was one of the first Jewish settlements outside the Old City. It faces the city ramparts across the Valley of Hell (Gehenna). After 1948, it lay very near the armistice line. For nearly twenty years it was within easy range of Jordanian snipers and was not a

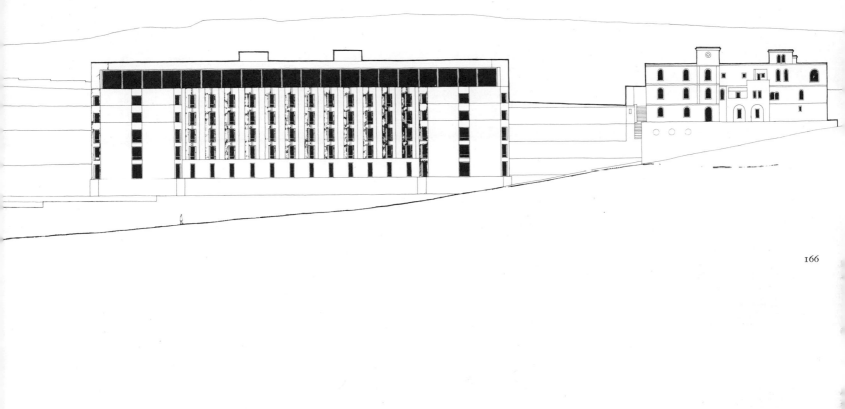

166

167

166 Elevation of the luxury hotel which was not
granted a building permit. Architect: Resnik.

167 Elevation of the original ensemble of buildings
now partially destroyed by the developer, Shimon
Maimon Peres.

168 View of the New National Park outside the Jaffa Gate—a kind of Cecil B. de Mille biblical set.

safe place to live. It was therefore populated by eccentric artists, and by the poor. After 1967, the authorities recognized that the settlement was a potential foreign currency gold mine; if properly renovated, its village charm and prime location would attract swarms of the rich and the cultured. Its old residents, who had lived through twenty years of danger, were not to be allowed to enjoy Yemin Moshe in peacetime, they naturally had to be removed. Many were evicted with token compensation; a few of the more stubborn still remain. In the meantime, Yemin Moshe is being converted into an 'artists' colony' for very well-to-do artists. Municipal authorities proudly show the renovated village to visitors as an example of how they are preserving Jerusalem's heritage.

Thus, the official housing and financial policies have the effect of encouraging the powerful and the privileged to exercise their power and privilege at the expense of the general public and particularly at the expense of the poor and the weak. Supposedly the benefits of this exercise of special privilege will

eventually reach the masses, and will reimburse the community for what was taken from it. Meanwhile, the social polarization which was supposed to be reduced by these policies is in fact being intensified.

### The Monsters that fell

During the course of their investigation of the city's plans, the members of the Urban Planning Unit came to the conclusion that unless there were a decisive reversal of major planning policies and decisions, there could be no town-planning in Jerusalem in the normally accepted sense of the word. It was clear that drastic action had to be taken.

Official municipal policy requires that prior to the stage of final deposition, planning decisions are to be kept secret. Everyone involved in preparing town-planning schemes or in reviewing building projects for the Jerusalem Municipality is bound by the 'secrecy clause' of the Municipality's employment contract. The 'secrecy clause' is designed to prevent speculators from taking unfair advantage of leaked information, and also to guarantee that town plans are formulated objectively, without pressure, serving public rather than private interests. But speculative developers in fact play a decisive role in formulating high level planning decisions and are thus usually much better informed about secret plans than any municipal employee.

The secrecy clause is used instead to prevent the public from deriving an undue advantage from premature knowledge of town-planning information. In order to break the vicious circle which had developed in the city's town-planning, the clause had to be ignored.

## Public Action

If Jerusalem's future were left only to the politicians and the builders, there would indeed be cause for despair. Politics are a dialogue of pressure and response: politicians attempt to formulate workable policies out of the pressures to which they are subjected. As long as these pressures are one-sided, the policies will necessarily only reflect specific and private notions of the general good. A counter-force must be brought to bear to fill out the political dialogue. In Jerusalem this counter-force has arisen, and it represents the hope of the city's future. The counterforce is of course an informed and active public. Although it may at times make politicians uncomfortable, public pressure is a necessary, legitimate and usually beneficial part of the planning process.

For quite some time the people of Jerusalem had been uncomfortably aware that the city's beauty and character were being eroded by the policies and projects which have been described. However the public had no way of expressing its dismay about the form that the city was taking. The lack of directly elected representatives in the Municipal Council and the national parliament, and the consensus politics of Israel's coalition government made a direct political expression of these feelings difficult. The role of the opposition, missing in the Israeli government, is often taken over by the Press. It was the Press, along with Israeli radio and television, which began to articulate the widespread concern of the public, and to provide it with detailed planning

information. In addition, the first built examples of town-planning by political and speculative fiat were providing incontrovertible visual evidence that the authorities had been disregarding the community's basic values in their decisions. The public forces gathered momentum, and shortly the politicians were faced with a formidable and angry pressure group. Immediately, decisions began to improve, errors were admitted, and some even reversed. There are in fact few cities in the world which can equal Jerusalem's planning record in that respect.

The public protest over the Omaria scheme began the process. The protest started when illustrations of a planning scheme on public open space in central Jerusalem were leaked to the public in contravention of the 'secrecy clause'. A *Jerusalem Post* article describes how Omaria became the focus of effective public action: '"It would make French Hill", said the mayor, "look like the Taj Mahal by comparison." This was the reaction of Teddy Kollek to his first view of a Housing Ministry model of its plans for the Omaria plot. These plans – calling for eight residential towers and two large hotels – came to be viewed by many who saw them as potentially the Housing Ministry's greatest blunder in Jerusalem. (The Ministry's French Hill development was conceded even by Housing Minister Ze'ev Sharef to have been

169

169  Plan of Yemin Moshe (J) and the National Park (I).

170  View of Yemin Moshe from Mount Zion.

170

113

171 The Omaria Tower. A Government-backed project built by private developers on public open space without a building permit. Architect: Dan Etan.

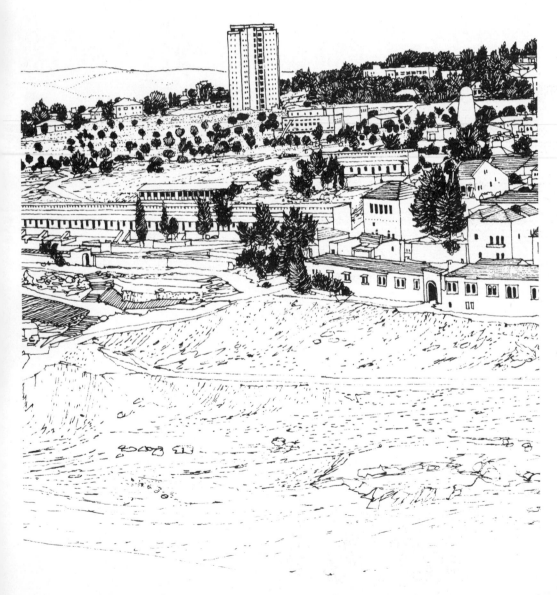

171

a mistake.) The Municipality and Mayor Kollek, however, have considerable explaining to do about their own role in the Omaria story. The solitary sixteen-storey tower that has already been erected at one end of the plot is almost universally regarded as a violent intrusion on the landscape, if not a desecration. The luxury apartment building shatters the skyline, blocks the view from a number of points, is completely out of scale with its tranquil surroundings and has become a visual focal point Jerusalem might better have reserved for some nobler symbol. The building now so generally condemned was constructed under the aegis of the Housing Ministry and with the tacit consent of the Municipality but without a building permit. Although it has lately begun a crack-down on illegal balconies and other minor additions to apartments, the Municipality made no attempt to stop the construction of the fifty-metre tall Omaria tower. Municipal officials say the building had been approved in principle by the District Commission and only lacked "formal" approval. An informed source claims that "formal" approval is lacking not because of a technicality, as the Municipality implies, but because of the basic failure of the responsible Government authorities to submit plans for the Omaria plot to the public – as required by law. It is this step – deposition – which permits neighbours and others who might be aggrieved by a scheme to raise objections. The District Planning Commission would then consider these objections before deciding on final approval, amendment, or rejection of the plan. "Democracy depends on such 'technicalities'," said the source. "*Habeas corpus* is also a technicality."' (*Jerusalem Post Weekend Magazine*, 'The towers of Omaria: building a mistake?' by Abraham Rabinovich.)

A public symposium was called by the Council for Beautiful Israel to discuss the plans for the rest of Omaria. These plans would cover the remaining site, the most important open space in the centre of the city, with additional luxury towers and hotels. Sketches, which had been prepared from the secret plans, were shown for the first time to the public.

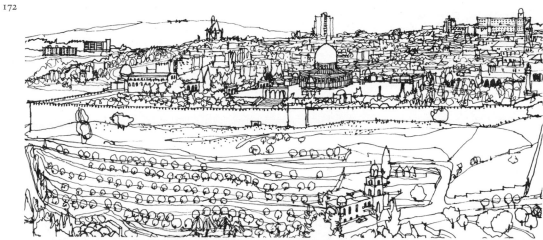

172

173

172  The Omaria Tower seen from Mount Scopus.

173  Scheme for the Omaria area (K). Also shown are the Commodore Hotel (M) and the King David Hotel annexe (L).

174  The original proposal for Omaria: a cluster of residential tower blocks and two luxury hotels. The Commodore Hotel appears on the right. Most of the scheme will not be built. *Overleaf* ➤

'The wrath of the audience rose on seeing (these) sketches. Some proposed campaigns of harassment of responsible officials. Some demanded court action. Some proposed demonstrations. Some attacked the Council for Beautiful Israel for not being militant enough. Some started collecting signatures for action committees.' (*Jerusalem Post*, 7 January 1972.) Public action had begun. It was concerted and passionate. Thousands of cards and letters were sent to officials. A demonstration was held with schoolchildren planting trees on the site of the proposed towers. A press and television campaign was undertaken. In the face of this vigorous action, the official plans simply withered away. The scheme for the additional towers was dropped and the area is for the present at least to remain open.

The public coalition which had achieved this remarkable success was an improbable mixture of left-wing students and right-wing extremists, new immigrants and veteran residents, religious fanatics and atheists, solid citizens and eccentric artists. Ultimately the coalition came to include Jews and Arabs. It was in fact a cross-section of the city's population mosaic, and was motivated by the one force which unites all of Jerusalem's divergent communities: a clear and powerful awareness of her special quality.

## The King David Hotel

A scheme for the King David Hotel Annexe suffered a fate similar to that of the Omaria Project. The plan for a twenty-two-storey tower block near the Old City had received legal approval, and an excavation license had already been issued. Sketches of the scheme were published. 'Within a few days of its

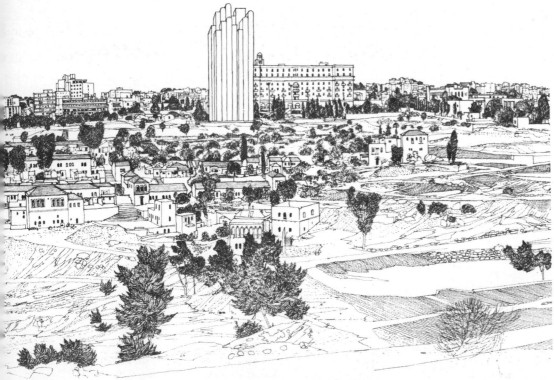

175 The proposed King David Hotel annexe, here seen from Abu-Tor, has been reduced to four storeys.

176 The project viewed from Mount Zion. Architect: Resnik.

publication, the head of the hotel firm announced that the plan had been abandoned. "I wouldn't rest quietly in my grave if people said I ruined Jerusalem," he declared.' (*Jerusalem Post*, 1 September 1972.)

One of the keys to the success of these actions was that proposed buildings were presented to the public in a way in which the visual relation of the project to the rest of the city could be immediately grasped. Since Jerusalem is a city of panoramas, an obvious device was to superimpose a proposed building upon its panoramic context. In this manner, the advice of architectural experts could be dispensed with, and ordinary citizens could be allowed to judge the suitability of projects themselves. Their taste has invariably proved superior to that of the experts.

## The Hyatt House Hotel

The story of the Hyatt House Hotel proposed for Mount Scopus is the most recent and dramatic example of what the public can achieve if it is aware of the implications of a project. 'For three years, the idea of a massive twenty-three storey building hardly drew a public murmur. So sanguine were the investors that they applied for, and received, permission to send in bulldozers to prepare the site and held a "cornerstone laying" ceremony last November with Tourism Minister Moshe Kol. Last May, a week before the District Planning Commission was to give final legal approval (a sketch was produced) showing how the hotel would look from a hilltop south of the Old City. It was seen to completely dominate the Dome of the Rock and the Temple Mount. The sketch appeared in that week's Friday editions of the *Jerusalem Post* and *Maariv*. There was an almost audible public gasp. The following Tuesday, a few hours before the District Commission was to assemble, its chairman, Rafi Levi, received a telephone call from Interior Minister Yosef Burg informing him that the political pressure for the building was off, and that a decision should be made on planning merits alone. The call was followed up by one from the chairman

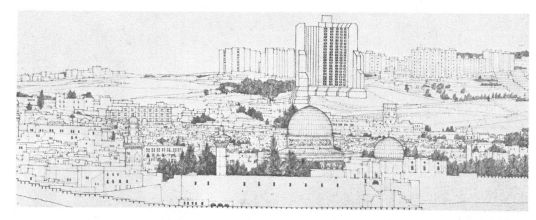

Architect Art Kutcher's sketch of the Old City sky line shows a 24-storey Hyatt House Hotel dominating Mount Scopus.

# HIGH, WIDE AND . . .

The latest planning controversy in Jerusalem centres on a proposal for a high-rise hotel on the lower slope of Mount Scopus which, its critics say, would change the character of the historic hill and become the dominant element in the environs of the Old City. The hotel architects say the building would enrich the skyline. ABRAHAM RABINOVICH reports.

177

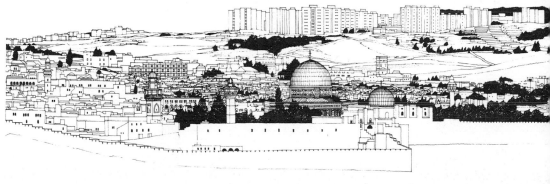

178

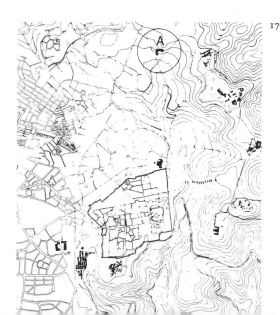

179

177  The Hyatt House Hotel to the north of the Old City, from an article in the *Jerusalem Post Weekend Magazine* by Abraham Rabinovich.

178  The hotel site seen from the Mount of Evil Counsel.

179  Location map of the Hyatt House Hotel at A. Architect: Micha Yerimitsky.

119

of the (Parliamentary) Interior Committee, expressing his concern over the proposal and asking him that a decision be postponed. Levi complied. Within four days of publication of the sketch, a multi-million dollar project with powerful political backing had ground to a halt.' (From the *Jerusalem Post Magazine* article by Abraham Rabinovich, 1 September 1972.) Permission for the project was subsequently refused, and the Municipal Council imposed a four-storey height limit on the site

The success of these public actions demonstrates that government policies and projects need not be accepted fatalistically. They can be changed, even if they have already been finally approved. The past successes create an obligation to continue action on a wider scale. The twenty-six high-rise projects already approved for central Jerusalem necessitate this wider scale of action.

## Alternative Approaches

The public controversy about the Hyatt House Hotel, in addition to preventing an architectural blunder, also compelled the Jerusalem Municipality to state clearly its high building policy for the Old City area, and for the entire city. The Municipality now accepts the principle that high buildings are not to be allowed in the immediate vicinity of the Old City. The further question of a city-wide high building policy is more difficult for the authorities to answer, since so many projects have already been approved in an *ad hoc* manner. The municipal government has not yet conceded that there may be an alternative approach. However, a review of the effects of high buildings should make it clear that such projects are not an economically, visually nor environmentally viable solution to the problems of building Jerusalem.

180 The Plaza and Commodore Hotels from Abu-Tor. The Plaza is under construction and the Commodore has received planning approval.

181 The Commodore and the Plaza from the Mount of Olives.

## High Buildings and Open Spaces

The notion, generally accepted by municipal officials everywhere, that high buildings allow the most efficient and economic use of land is usually false. The effect of 'peripheral blight' and excessive traffic generation have been mentioned. The social costs arising from these effects, the time loss and inconvenience, the pollution and environmental deterioration, are not normally included in the municipal calculations, nor are the financial and social costs of the demolition and new road construction which high density projects necessitate. High building projects also have the effect of actually forcing those activities out of the centre which most belong there, and replacing them with functions and activities which have no need to be in the centre, and which unnecessarily congest its streets with commuter traffic. The activities which make a city centre attractive and viable are those which involve face-to-face contacts: retail shopping, cafés and restaurants, small offices dealing directly with the public, trades and professional services; in short those activities which are usually not prepared to pay the high rents associated with high density projects. These functions are replaced by clerical and administrative ones, whose large office-worker populations do not deal with the public, and could be more conveniently and economically accommodated in decentralized locations. Thus these projects are seldom rational from a town-planning point of view, nor are they in the least economic for the city. Beyond the fact that high buildings realize speculative expectations, the primary motive behind them is corporate prestige.

The studies done by the planners for Jerusalem's central business district have shown that there is no functional or economic justification for high buildings in the city's centre, and that the commercial needs of the city can be more efficiently accommodated in lower structures. Those mistakes which have been built should be left, and not added to. The appropriate concept of a centre for Jerusalem is one whose density and scale are carefully related to those of the Old City, and to the

real functional and economic needs of the entire city, rather than to the current financial difficulties of the Municipality. The concept of the centre is also tied to the development of an open space and pedestrian system which links the city's residential

182 View from the Mount of Olives of some of the 26 high-rise projects which have municipal backing, planning permission or building licences. From left to right: the Commodore Hotel; the Plaza Hotel, Beit Ha'am, Beit Midot and the Alliance project. '*Is this the city that men call the perfection of beauty, the joy of the whole earth?*'

neighbourhoods both to the Old City area and to the commercial core. This system takes its form not from an artificially imposed geometry, but from the givens of the topography, and from the character of Jerusalem's panoramic views. The landscape of the Old City is Jerusalem's heritage, to be passed on to future generations. The beauty of her landscape, its soils, its rocks, its vegetation, is complete. It needs no further elaboration.

Jerusalem's open spaces provide her visual structure. The city is now undergoing that period of rapid growth which will stamp her character for centuries. Visionary decisions are required at this point in her history. To reduce

the city's key open spaces at this crucial stage to accommodate hotels and luxury flats is a disastrous and unnecessary mistake. Economic surveys have shown that the demand for luxury hotel accommodation over the next fifteen years will be filled by hotels now existing and being built. Adequate sites for smaller hotels exist and have been pointed out to the authorities.

## Growth Rates

The speed and extent of the transfer of governmental functions from Tel Aviv to Jerusalem will to a large extent determine the city's rate of growth. Other growth rates, such as that

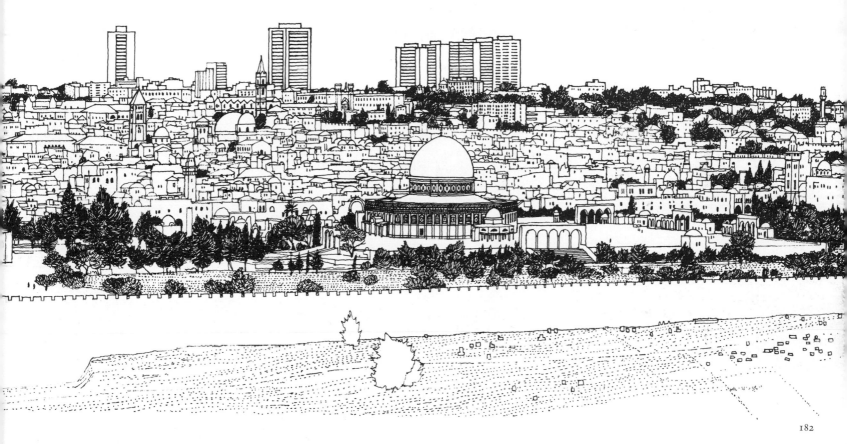

182

of tourism, are not being based upon a realistic appraisal of capacities, but on a programme to promote unlimited expansion.

Jerusalem cannot absorb the rapid rate of urban growth which is artificially being forced upon her. Instead of continuing this policy, priority should be given to accommodating Jerusalem's real social and human needs: new housing should be constructed to thin out existing over-crowding; resources should be devoted to the renovation of the city's existing building stock, and efforts should be made to rectify past housing mistakes, rather than to build new ones.

The city's rates of population growth, of commercial expansion, and of tourism are not natural laws, they are the function of government policies. Until recently, these policies generally ignored Jerusalem's special qualities, the physical limitations of the site and the will of her residents. Recent events have shown that Jerusalem's citizens have the power to influence these decisions, and they are now using this power. The common awareness of Jerusalem's realities, of her landscape and of her historical continuity, are among the forces that have brought this about.

Architects in Jerusalem often complain that they are not allowed the freedom to express fully the spirit of our age, and its technology.

In fact, Western technology has invaded Jerusalem and is sometimes being used, and proposed, with very little restraint. But Western culture has another contribution to make to the city's cumulative history. This contribution does not involve the imposition of alien forms upon her, for it is bound up with a respect for her past and a love for her special beauty. The contribution is a spiritual one – the best part of the heritage of the West: that people can freely and commonly determine their collective future. This is another expression of Jerusalem's ancient theme, coming back to her, and it will, like its predecessors, leave its mark upon the Holy City.

# Epilogue: the Jerusalem Committee
# June 1973

*'Jerusalem must not let opportunism rule. Make this clear to those who think they can rule the world by jingling money in their pockets.'*

Louis I. Kahn

*'. . . there was deep concern over practices and procedures that had not changed since 1970. In a final resolution the [Jerusalem] committee expressed "unqualified condemnation" of the new skyscrapers marring the skyline. It urged that plans approved for other high-rise buildings be scrapped, with developers compensated for their expenses.'*

Harry Trimborn
*The Los Angeles Times*
4 July, 1973

*'. . . the committee's final resolution expressed concern "over the continuing lack of clarity in the hierarchy of decision-making" and the inability to work out firm policies on vital planning issues which could be converted into a legally binding plan. A committee member said privately that obscurity of responsibility was not accidental but a well known method of avoiding blame. "They put up two extra storeys on the King David, build the Plaza Hotel in the park, put up the Omariya tower – all the authorities say it's a mistake and shrug their shoulders. There's no one to blame because you don't know who made the decision".'*

Abraham Rabinovich
*The Jerusalem Post*
27 June, 1973

*'The campaign against high-rise construction received an influential boost last week from the Jerusalem Committee. . . . In a resolution adopted after several hours of animated debate, the committee expressed "unqualified condemnation" of the high-rise buildings already constructed within sight of the Old City. It also called for a halt to the projects already approved, for compensation for the builders and the adoption of the eight-storey maximum as official policy. . . . This . . . would respect the topography of Jerusalem and avoid surrounding the Old City with what Mr [Buckminster] Fuller called the "high-rise walls of greed".'*

Terence Smith
*The New York Times*
26 June, 1973

The Mayor of Jerusalem pledged himself to implement the committee's resolution, including the reversal of and compensation for high-rise projects already approved. Although construction in Jerusalem has been temporarily halted as a result of the October 1973 war, building plans have not been altered and the Mayor's pledge remains unfulfilled.

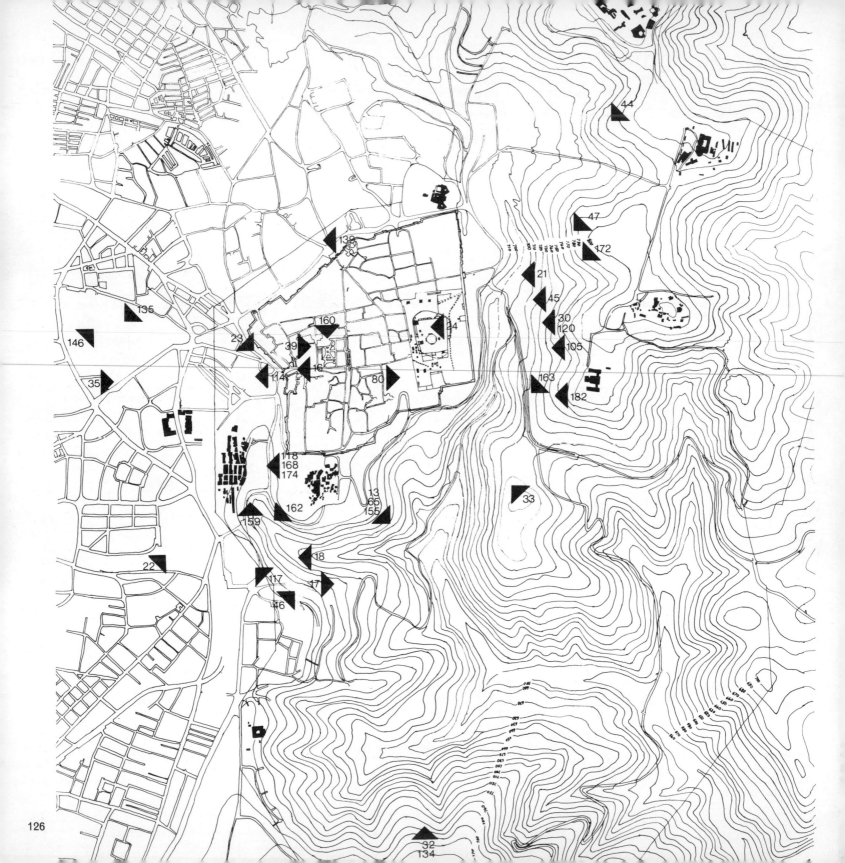

# Acknowledgments and Sources of Illustrations

The Author wishes to thank those Jerusalemites whose ideas are found throughout this book, and whose efforts have been instrumental in improving Jerusalem's town planning. Among them are Shlomo Aronson, Mike Turner, David Fields, Yehuda Haezrachi, Yuval Elizur, Ester Niv-Krendel, Peter Bugod, Colin Frank, and Yochanan Minsker.

Michelle Cartlidge and Ruth Behr have given valuable graphic assistance. Permission to reproduce some of the author's drawings has been kindly granted by the Ministry for Religious Affairs, State of Israel, and by the Supreme Muslim Council, Jerusalem.

The following books have been useful in providing reference material: *Jerusalem, Rock of Ages* by Fosco Maraini with photos by Alfred Bernheim, *Roman Architecture* by Gilbert Picard, *The City as an Image of Man* by T. C. Stewart, *Design of Cities* by Edmund Bacon, *A History of Architectural Styles* by Fritz Baumgart, *Mies van der Rohe* by Werner Blaser, *The Holy Land in Old Prints and Maps* by Zev Vilnay, *This is Jerusalem* by Menashe Har El, and *A Concise History of Western Architecture* by R. Furneaux Jordan. The quotation from Erich Neumann's book *The Origins and History of Consciousness* is used by kind permission of Routledge and Kegan Paul, Ltd.

183 Key map locating the urban and landscape views in and around the Old City which appear in this book. The numbers refer to the drawings in which the views are illustrated.

1 After Vilnay, *The Holy Land in Old Prints and Maps*
2 The Jerusalem Master Plan Office
20 Courtesy of the Ministry for Religious Affairs, State of Israel
25 Courtesy of the Ministry for Religious Affairs, State of Israel
28 After a British Mandatory survey map
33 From a photograph by Dalia Klemes
37 After an 18th century engraving in Edmund Bacon, *Design of Cities*.
38 From an 18th century engraving
51 After Banister Fletcher, *A History of Architecture on the Comparative Method*
53 After Picard, *Living Architecture: Roman*
54 After a plan in 'Architecture in Israel', *Journal of the Association of Engineers and Architects in Israel*, October 1968
55 After a plan by H. Frankfort in Baumgart, *A History of Architectural Styles*
56 After a plan by Brunner-Traut and Hell in Jordan, *A Concise History of Western Architecture*
57 After a plan by H. Koepf in Baumgart, *A History of Architectural Styles*
58 After a plan in 'Architecture in Israel', *Journal of the Association of Engineers and Architects in Israel*, October 1968
59 After a plan in Baumgart, *A History of Architectural Styles*
61 After a photograph in Picard, *Living Architecture: Roman*
62 By kind permission of the Supreme Muslim Council, Jerusalem
66 Courtesy of the Ministry for Religious Affairs, State of Israel
68 After survey by Captain Charles Warren, RE, 1867
70 After a reproduction in Vilnay, *The Holy Land in Old Prints and Maps*
71 After a drawing of 1362 in Amico, *Plans of the Sacred Edifices of the Holy Land*
72 After a French drawing of the 15th century in Vilnay, *The Holy Land in Old Prints and Maps*
74 After an Italian map of 1588, in Amico, *Plans of the Sacred Edifices of the Holy Land*
75 After a drawing in Amico, *Plans of the Sacred Edifices of the Holy Land*

76 After a drawing in 'Architecture in Israel', *Journal of the Association of Engineers and Architects in Israel*, October 1968
77 After a print of about 1830 in Vilnay, *The Holy Land in Old Prints and Maps*
78 After a pictorial map of 1875 in Vilnay, *The Holy Land in Old Prints and Maps*
79 After a drawing by Shemuel Shulman, 1887
81–87 After maps by Israel Kimchi
93 After a photograph by J. W. Baxtresser in Jordan, *A Concise History of Western Architecture*
95 After a plan in Edmund Bacon, *Design of Cities*
96 After a photograph in 'Paris, Bloody Paris', *Sunday Times*, 17 November 1972
97 After a plan in Baumgart, *A History of Architectural Styles*
98 After a photograph by S. J. Brandon in Jordan, *A Concise History of Western Architecture*
99 After a photograph from the USIS
100 After a photograph by Penelope Reed, in Jordan, *A Concise History of Western Architecture*
101 After a photograph by Lingauer, in Jordan, *A Concise History of Western Architecture*
129 After a map by Israel Kimchi
138 After the Ordnance Survey of Great Britain
140 Proposal by the author and Shlomo Aronson made for the Central Business District Plan
143 Proposal by the author and Shlomo Aronson for the Central Business District Plan
144 After the map of the Outline Town Plan for the Old City area
153 After the legal zoning map
157 After the map published in *The Old City and its Environs, Outline Townplanning Scheme 1970*, by the Jerusalem Committee
177 From an article by Abraham Rabinovich, *Jerusalem Post*, 18 May 1972
183 Courtesy of the Ministry for Religious Affairs, State of Israel

With the exception of the following, all illustrations are by the author:

1, 9, 23, 28, 37, 63, 67, 70, 72, 74, 77, 78, 79 by Michelle Cartlidge
48, 49, 51, 76, 137, 138, 153, 154 by Ruth Behr
157, 179 by Margaret Leppard

# Index